BORN WITH A VISION

A Gift of Love

TITUS R. NGATEH

Contents

Dedication

I want to dedicate this book the victims of the Liberian and Sierra Leone's Civil War, including those who have gone through this kind of tumult in the past, or even now as I am writing. It is because of the suffering and the pain we all share in common that brought this vision to light.

To those of us who lost precious family members, friends and loved ones, God is our only consoler. I will always love as we share this trip of painful memories together. We found love and joy in our misfortune through the support of those who took their time to walk us through the process of grief.

I believe those of us who are still alive after the chaos have found courage, strength, and redemption in the midst of our loses and disparity. Above all, I like to thank God for those who have become part of my life over the years. You mean so much to me.

Now I am delivering the finished product of this story of our frustrations and sorrows during and after the conflicts to you and the world. God bless you.

Acknowledgements

I could not have written this book without the support of my family. To my late parents, my father Robert Saah Bendu and my lovely mother Nessie Sia for giving me the greatest gift of knowing God as my Lord and savior since my childhood. You serve as an inspiration to me and have taught me to love and respect people at all times and to serve mankind. You taught me to put humility above material gain and selfish interests. I could not have done it without you.

To my wonderful uncle, Thomas and his beloved wife, Nessie, I appreciate everything you did for me. You took over where my parents left off. You became my parents overnight and taught me what it takes to make a difference in the lives of others.

To Uncle Edwin Temba who was killed by a few men from his own ethnic group in 1987, you were funny, brave, hardworking and a master of many trades. You told me to get the best education I could in life. I will always miss you. To my brothers Jeff, Nehemiah, and Hallie, and my sisters Helen, Finda, and Tawah, thanks for being there for me with your love, support, and prayers.

To my sons, Titus S. Jr. and Jeremiah, as well as my daughter, Moriah, who was born when I was about to complete this book, you are the best gifts I received from God. To my late younger brother, Marcus who died of diabetes in 1987, my older brother, Junior, and my uncle, Nyumah Ree, both killed in the Liberian Civil War, and to my late sister, Hannah, we miss you! My lovely aunt Christina, I am thankful for the times you held and nourished me. You will be missed. Aunt Finda, you are an instrument of courage to me. Thank for your prayers.

Thank you, Sis Fata and your husband Mohammed, who sponsored my resettlement to the United States of America; my best friend and brother, James Kwesi and the late Nancy, known as Weedor, you were the woman whose love for me had no end; my daughter Marie Massary, our bond is for a lifetime. I love you from the bottom of my heart. To my friends and other family members who have been there for me, thank you. I am grateful to Andrew for taking his personal time to critique and edit portion of this manuscript and Tiffiny for being a friend who also contributed to this project. Special thanks to all the other editors who contributed.

Time and space could not permit me to mention your names. I love you all and wish you God's greatest blessing.

When you look up in the sky,
there are many stars.
Some are high others are low.
Beyond them are many more elements.
Why settle for less when God has given us the
mind to accomplish not only good, but great things

Introduction

The story of this book is my life; the book began as things in my life evolved and with my desire to simply record the incidents in my diary as they played out in my life. My story begins with my time as a refugee in Guinea, between 1993 and 2001.

As a social worker immediately out of high school I worked with refugees from Liberia and Sierra Leone until 2001, recording all of my experiences in my diary. These experiences provided an opportunity to not only grow personally in my relationship with God, but an opportunity for me to bring hope through encouragement to those with broken dreams and who had lost hope. I was able to help by motivating and encouraging other refugees to dream, to renew their minds and to pursue their goals and achieve their dreams. The journey was tumultuous, but through faith and a belief in the possibilities of change; many of us left the dungeons that had held them for so long.

After high school, eager to pursue a career and gradually becoming successful and seeing the direction of my life take shape, my anticipation was high. In spite of my schooling and many travels, I could not have ever had expected that, through all the tribulations and disappointments experienced through my life, I would have taken such a turn that I would become a writer. Many of the refugees questioned their current circumstances and the reason having to endure such hardship, and none of us believed that we deserve such tribulation. However, through and abiding faith and belief, God delivered us from what was seen as sorrow, and then propel many of us into success.

Many years later, in 2003, I found myself in the United Stated looking back through those diaries that held stories of so much tribulation and pain. Through those torn pages and the clips that held it all together, I was moved to tears, I knew that this story had to be told; told because it attests to the grace of God and the mercy of a loving Father. No; the memories were not all good ones, but throughout all the bitter times, there were so many ways in which God revealed Himself and took us through those hardships.

The civil war raged through Liberia and Sierra Leone, families were torn apart and many lost hope and became bitter. Many were without a way of escaping, but God's unfailing grace keep many, and I write my story to encourage and to empower others to press on and never give up on God. My experiences have haunted me every day and night, and I realized that it was my assignment to write this and to encourage others to never give up. Read, enjoy, and learn. Thank God, it is in your hand.

Life with my Parents

I believe this is the right time to sit down and share my life; with the world. Life as a child was full of excitement, and those few years were some of the best times of my life. One would be curious to know why those years were special and meaningful to me as a child. There was a big world out there, but I knew little. I did not understand what it was all about, but it awaited me like any other kid. A child brought into the world today faces the same problems of this life.

I am the second of five boys. I lived with my parents in a peaceful community in Liberia. My dad, a dedicated man, worked hard to provide for us. My mother supported him in every possible way. Together, my parents worked to see us mature and to become productive adults in order for them to reap the benefits of their labor when they grew old.

My dad had a college education. He served as a secretary for a local organization in our community. He also served as a deacon at the community Pentecostal Church where my family worshipped. I was too young to understand my father's role as a deacon in the church. At the church, the kids went to a separate church school, apart from the adults.

Dad made sure we were at church every Sunday. He wanted the best for us. My father wanted his children's future to be bright. He worked hard to make sure we were secured financially, and made sure we had a good education.

On special Sundays such as Easter, Thanksgiving and Christmas, we all worshipped together. Of course, we were placed in separate pews with adult supervision so we would not disrupt services. I enjoyed the choir singing!

The church had two choirs; One English and the other ethnic. The English choir wore pretty gowns and sang from hymn books. The ethnic choir used traditional instruments and sang in our ethnic tongue of Kissi. Members of that choir always wore shining African attire. It was wonderful to watch them perform. They always lifted the spirit of the church with dances and chants. My mother sang in that choir.

I was never a shy kid. I played with other kids at church. Sunday school teacher played the guitar and the kids sang along with him. I enjoyed Sunday school especially Bible stories. I was always on time for Sunday school and when it was time for the teacher to tell the Bible stories, I sat still and listened carefully. The story of David and Goliath captivated me. Those who answered the teacher's questions were given prizes at the end of Sunday school. On some Sundays, I won toy cars, trucks and planes. No one won or brought toy guns to Sunday school.

Our church was located in the red light district of Monrovia. It seated about 500 hundred members. It was fenced in to protect members' automobiles and to keep kids from running into approaching traffic. The church yard was beautiful. It was surrounded by pretty red and yellow flowers. On Sunday mornings, one could hear a pin drop because everyone went to church.

The church was several hundred yards from the Atlantic Ocean and the pretty sandy beaches had attracted many foreign nationals to the area. When we drove to church in the morning, we could hear the waves of the sea beating against the shores. It was not unusual to see people walking on the beach during the morning hours. After Sunday services, Dad took me and other family members to walk on the beach.

Sunday morning, kids played football (soccer) in the streets because there were fewer cars on the streets and my family rode a cab to church. My cab driver had to watch out for those kids when he drove down the streets.

At the church, we heard news of those ill at home. We also heard about those who had lost loved ones. There was news about those who were engaged to be married and those who traveled out of the country. Those who did not attend church missed out on the news in the community.

After church, Mom and Dad took us to visit aunts, nieces, nephews and uncles. I always had fun visiting other relatives. It was fun and exciting meeting other kids. Those visits brought the family closer together.

I loved living with Mom and Dad. They taught me much about life. Dad talked about the importance of a good education. He believed that a good education was guaranteed security to success in life.

Dad's sudden death dramatically changed the family. Mom took me and my brothers to live with grandma on a nearby rubber plantation once the funeral ended. I angrily demanded to leave because the man Mom was dating was a drunk. He physically and verbally abused Mom in our presence. I could not stand to look at this drunken man insult my mom.

Then one day, Mom took me to live with my aunt and later with my paternal uncle. I was unprepared for the changes. In a span of four years, I had lived with my mom; an uncle, and an aunt. As the years dragged on, I felt sad and at times insecure. I was in an unfamiliar environment with relatives I did not know well. I may remember these changes for a while. I can safely assume that there are kids out there who may be going through similar changes as I did.

I will always cherish the memories of Mom and Dad. They were always there for us. They taught us to treat others with love and respect. My dad was a caring and loving person. He touched the lives of those who knew him. He also taught us to care for others. He always said, "If you want others to treat you right, then treat them right. If you do, you will succeed in life. Of course, people don't always treat kids right."

The world is full of challenges. It can be a sad place to live at times, but it is always good to have hope, even in the midst of civil wars as in Liberia and Sierra Leone. Off course, people suffer when their leaders make bad decisions.

Life is unpredictable. One never knows what tomorrow may bring. It is always better to live one day at a time.

Mom said Daddy was organized. He prepared for the future and he wanted the best for his family, including those around him. His office was always neat. Everything was in order. He took time out to help others in the community. He also helped the church to organize events. After his death, we wondered who would replace Dad to do all the things he used to do.

My parents were happy together. They took us for haircuts, shopping and visits to friends. Suddenly Dad was gone! Mom was unprepared to care for us. She struggled to provide for our needs. Mother lacked formal education and, with no income, she was unable to support all of us. She also wanted peace of mind. Thank God she was a praying mother! She always gathered us together when things got rough. Mother taught us to be strong and hold on to each other. She always assured us that things would be better. Mother was a strong believer. She always had her faith fixed on the Lord. God continues to be the strength of our family.

We had trouble believing that Dad was dead. We thought he would come back. Time went on and, as we grew older, we realized that Dad would never come back. He was gone forever.

Life now was different and difficult. Mom was there, but Dad had been the sole breadwinner of the family. We were never prepared for this change, and I believe Mom was not prepared either. The days became weeks, the weeks became months, and the months became years, and we began to slowly accept the challenges and the changes. We had to accept what life has dealt our family in order to survive what lay ahead for us. It was unexpected, but we had to find meanings, even in the midst of the tragedy.

Mom felt uneasy living in the house where her husband died. She said, "Sometimes, I feel your father's presence with me. He seems to be telling me to be strong and learn to raise you all by myself."

Mom had to leave her home and move in with grandma at a nearby rubber plantation. She thought this was the best decision for the family temporarily. We had to leave other relatives and friends behind to resettle to find comfort. Those memories were difficult to forget.

Shortly after Dad's death, Mom started dating. Somehow, I was different from my siblings as a child. For some reason, I knew Mom was headed for trouble. I felt uneasy about taking on a stepfather so soon. Frankly, I had no control over the decision. I was very young to understand everything about feelings, especially concerning Mom.

Mom's relationship with her boyfriend now became a problem for us. The man was drunk on many occasions. When he got drunk, it was difficult getting the attention we needed from him. In that state of mind, he could not function as the man mother thought he was. I could not stop him, but I expressed my feelings that he could not continue to treat my mom, and my siblings the way he did.

Our dad was a loving and caring man. Here, we were dealing with another difficult situation not long after Dad's passing. I felt helpless because I could not do anything to change the situation. I did not know what to do to avoid this man.

Dad had left some money in the bank for family emergencies, and for our education. Mom was not aware that it would cost a lot of money to send five kids to school. Unfortunately, her boyfriend could not see far enough ahead to understand that it would take good parenting skills and better financial planning to educate me and my younger brothers. Alcoholism leads to many other problems. Mom wanted to help this important man in her life, but she could not figure out a way to do so. She seemed helpless as well as unwilling to get away from him.

I saw no future living with Mom and her boyfriend at the time. I prayed that one day God would show me the way. God understood our problems. Soon after, I returned to Monrovia to live with my aunt. I had to get away to get peace of mind. I had tried so hard to stay, but something inside me kept saying it was time to go. I had to leave; it was my call. I left Mom and three younger brothers behind. It was a sad day when I left. I had no clue what life would be like for them or for me. I was leaving, but would not forget them. Mom and her children seemed to be trapped in a situation they could not change.

Even as a kid, I was willing to wait for God's time. He would show me the way if I were patient to wait on Him, but at times I wondered if God was real, and was hearing my cry for help. Here I was, away from my mom and brothers trying hard to finding meanings in life at such an early age.

Wherever I went, I was determined to carry on my education. I knew Dad's advice to us about the importance of good education. He was not around anymore, but I was not going to let him down by dropping out of school. One of my greatest challenges was finding relatives to help to pay my school fees.

The decision to live with my aunt was a blessing. It was difficult in the beginning, but it proved to be the best decision I have ever made as a young man. From the day I left Mom and my siblings, I knew I had a huge task ahead of me. I had a goal to reach and a mission to accomplish, as I traveled through this world. I had no choice, but to keep pressing on and asking God for His protection.

In the City

Time slipped by quickly as life with aunt was different. I was away from my mother and step—dad. I was free to some degree, but Aunt had her own marital problems. I was young and could not fully understand her problem with her husband. I noticed that she was a quiet and reserved person who never said a lot, but she was friendly. She confided in her neighbors and her younger sister. Her friends and neighbors loved and embraced her friendship. They somehow understood her problem and tried to console her when she was in tears.

Aunt rested in her bed quietly and did not wish to be bothered after spending her day at the market where she conducted business activities. We kept silent not to disturb her while she slept. Some nights she woke up in the middle of the night and cried because of the manner in which her husband treated her.

When Aunt's husband was with his friends, he spoke softly and made jokes. When he returned home, he was a different man to her. Sure enough, I was young and lacked the knowledge to conclude what he really was. After a few years of living with Aunt, his neighbors said a lot about him. It was then I came to know the true story. I am not exaggerating how he treated Aunt. Something was not just right. They had four children, but one passed away. A few years went by and they were still together while I was away at school. Aunt got sick for a while. I don't know if her marital problems had anything to do with her health, may be and over the years the sadness, stress, and lack of will power to find a lasting remedy grew into depression. My aunt's marital problems may have made her vulnerable to other sicknesses, which could have led to her demise few years early. I guess there was no way out for her, in what seemed to be a love story.

He was a cab driver who was away from home most of the time. Could this have caused his strangeness or was it his affairs with other women from what the neighbors used to say? This was too much for Aunt. He made many excuses why he could not spend more time home with the family. My aunt confronted him about having affairs. They used to argue when I was around, about his infidelity. He used to spend some time at home when he brought money for food and other goodies his family needed. That was a good idea. She loved her husband. She wanted more attention and affection like any women. She needed his love but he could only do the little he could to show his love and affection when he felt the need to do so.

Aunt's friends kept her informed about his unfaithfulness, but she was very patient and never encouraged a fight. He was free like a bird. Divorce would ease her pain; early removal from this man was the answer, but such a move remains unacceptable in our culture, especially when children are involved. Family, friends, and elders privately appealed to her to stay and hang in there, with the hope that things would take a positive turn in Aunt's favor and restore her marriage. She remained firm on these things, despite the turmoil she experienced.

My aunt's younger sister visited us and tried to comfort her by spending time with her and mending her broken heart. Together, they visited families and friends. She hesitantly accepted at times to go with her younger sister but her sister's effort did not solve the problem. The love and attention she longed for from the man she loved became an illusion. While I was away in Guinea, seeking refuge from the Liberian Civil War, Aunt took sick and was pronounced dead after a few months. She had gone to rest in peace. My question is: what could have caused her death? Aunt's unhappiness, life's circumstances, or human nature-only time may tell. I felt her pain and mourned her early death. She was dead and gone. There was nothing we could do anymore. I regretted her death and will do so every day. If I knew what I know now and was of age, I could have intervened to offer help. There was nothing I could do to reverse this tragic loss. What is still on my mind is an appreciation for the little she did for me, even when she was so broken and could not function well, memories of how she came home to make food for us and later returned to the market without eating, still haunt me up to this day. She was a different person on the inside. Only God knew this woman and what she went through.

Looking back on her pain had strengthened me to find the meaning of life. News of her death hit me so hard; in Guinea where I went to seek refuge from the civil war. I was in search of a brighter future.

Almost three years had passed since I left my mother and brothers. My older brother lived my uncles in Monrovia. We frequently met when I lived with my aunt. We had a bond no one could break. We grew up in the same city, and we did almost everything together. We were best of friends, too. The smile on his face made it easier for him to get along with his peer group. The girls fought over him many times. He held no special girl in his heart. He spoke kind words and went about his business. They thought he was the person they wanted, but he was young. He was friendly to everyone he knew or met.

I did not know that the memory of my brother's death would change me forever. We had some things in common. Like my brother, girls were attracted to me and, like him; I was smooth and easy-going with no fighting or causing trouble. Those days determined the foundation for our future. Conditions also changed for the worst, and separated our family. It was the result of a brutal civil war in Liberia towards the end of the 20th century. The civil war intensified, and was right under our noses, but many ignored the warnings it embodied because the government claimed the situation was under control. We were disappointed in the deception that the government manufactured. Thousands of innocents paid the price with their lives because the government lied and prevented us from preparing for the worse that was imminent. We were surrounded by war on all sides with nowhere or place to hide. It became almost impossible to escape the city center without being trapped by warring factions. When the fighting finally descended on Monrovia, I saw brutality and some of the most horrific scenery of the civil war. Warring factions did not realize that we were all Liberians. Brothers killing their own brothers and sisters, and we were referring to them as freedom fighters. It was the worst kind of mistake Liberians made.

The once loving and peaceful Liberia become a training ground for human massacre. Liberia, a place where I experienced real peace and freedom of mind, had become a battlefield of blood. The only choice was to escape the fighting by any means necessary. That was exactly what many did. Here, I was leaving a society I had known all of my childhood life: friends, family, and loved ones. No one knew who would live to see the end of the civil war. I was departing, not willingly, but in order to live and realize God's purpose for my life. It seemed like a forceful exodus.

Abroad, one thing I sought was to find a true friend. I was not the only one in search of friends who shared my dreams, and fully accepted me for who I had become. Many are living in the midst of humans but some still find they are lonely and deserted by either someone they had counted on all their lives or that they can't still find out the true meaning of life. For the lucky ones, who understand the true meaning of life and know what it means for mankind to live in peace, they are like heroes who have found the right path in life.

Life could be simple, but you need to accept its reality and then you can somehow make it through. Life is an everyday process and so we all need some guidance to live a peaceful life where ever we may be. For some reason, it could take some time to find the right direction that leads to the real purpose for life. Some are fortunate to have the opportunity to understand how to accelerate life in the positive way. And that is a good thing. Life can be a mystery some times, but we have to keep searching to find the answers.

I had no way to survive in Monrovia with the fighting between the rebels and government troops continued. Everything was crazy. It was difficult to find food and there was no one to trust. Bodies were everywhere on the streets. You could hardly find any commercial transportation, law had broken down.

Cars that were seen on the streets were either government's vehicles or rebels. Many people wanted to leave the city center in order to avoid the fighting that both sides sought to descend on their own people. It was too late for many.

I, too, was among the unprepared and shaken p
to leave the city center and seek safety else were
portation, food, or safe drinking water, it made to
more difficult and dangerous. This was a do or di
and government troops occupied the way. Anyone could be killed at
any time or any moment. The choice to leave the capital city was as
risky as the attempt to seek refuge in the interior. The risk was determined when the journey began.

By this time, I was young. My level of thinking and risk–calculation was limited. Thanks to age I was not the head of the group at
this dangerous time, but the head of the group agreed that we leave
almost immediately from Monrovia by foot to Lofa.

Before the death of Aunt I was taken away and sent to Lofa to
live with one of my uncles. In Lofa, it was agreed among family
members that I live with uncle and his wife. The thing I wanted the
most was education. Life in Lofa took a different path that determined my future. Upon my arrival in the district of Foya, I was
faced with another life that was totally beyond my comprehension. I
would come to understand this environment later. It was good when
I learned I was leaving Aunt to return to Lofa to be with uncle.

To my surprise, I was taken to a remote village first. It was not
really that bad but I felt disappointed because I wanted to leave the
village early. It was another battle, between my surroundings and
me. But one question I kept asking myself was, "Am I guilty of
doing something?" I thought like a child and could not fathom the
ups and downs of the life at this time. I waited helplessly for uncle
to return and get me from the village and take me with him. It had
taken too long. In the process, I felt abandoned. My future, at the
time seemed oblique. I could not determine my future and what it

ould be in the next ten or twenty years ahead of me. I prayed and waited for answers.

As time went by, I ran out of patience and could not take it anymore. I felt lonely like someone trapped in a jungle wilderness and desperate to find a way out. I could not think of anything else to do. Here, I was doing nothing at all. I was a normal lad in school, living with my parents. Almost six months had disappeared just like that and I was not in school. I knew education was the key and needed that key. But the price to obtain this key was huge. I was prepared to make any sacrifice to get an education. I was young and had no means of helping myself.

My aunt, who brought me to the village to see some of our family members, had quickly returned to Monrovia, concluding that uncle was on his way to get me. My uncle, for some reason, did not come to get me from the village as early as I thought to ensure I return to school. I could not tell what has happened at this time. By then I missed school so much. This was the only thing I dreamed of.

I knew mother was now a widow. I had to depend on God to keep me strong to do something in order to improve our situation. This was my call. I prayed every day and night, waiting for God's answer. I waited long but nothing happened. I decided to take action. I had no right to force Uncle to take me away but I wanted to be educated to serve as a role model for others. I wanted to be in the position to offer something to those "who were less fortunate". I wanted them to have the kind of opportunity that I never had as a child. This thinking kept me alive and awake.

My immediate family had fallen apart. My childhood life was in shambles. I only traveled with a broken heart; my father was dead. We the children could not get the nurturing from him anymore. We did not have the presence of our mother, which became another problem. I was overwhelmed by frustration, sorrows and grief. "God" I would say, "you have taken my dad, and my mother is nowhere to be to be found. Who is going to look after me?" So I thought. But God was still in control.

The friends I left behind in Monrovia were in school and doing well. "What will my future be like? Where can I go to get the help I need? Who can I ask for help?" These were the questions I asked myself. I had no answers. I could not continue this way. "I will take upon myself go to meet uncle; "I said at one time.

It was a mission I could not afford to turn down. This was a possible mission. I had no clue where the will came from, but I felt the energy to do so. I left the village and reached uncle's house late one evening, but he had left to go to work. I met his wife, who was not sure what was going on. My third younger brother was already living with them. Joining the family meant another burden. But the truth was clear: I needed them at this very crucial time.

In Foya my plan was not to harm anyone or create problem for them. My intention was clear. I needed some sort of supervision – someone to help out at this critical time. I was starting life with Uncle, his wife, and other family members who were there to be helped.

My uncle's wife had three children from her previous marriage before she met and married Uncle. They were blessed with four other children. Uncle had few children of his own from past failed relationships. His wife made sure everything was taken care of at home with special attention to the younger children. It was the best thing to do. I was the late bloomer. I was prepared to accept any challenge in my way. I needed nothing more than education. With my uncle and his wife, I spent additional months without going to school. I was late for that semester. I was determined, willing, and persistent in my focus for education. I was patient. I did most of the work uncle's wife assigned me-to. She and I went many places and ran some business transactions together. I did what I could do as a child. Someday, she was gentle to me; other times she was hard on me. I was young and thought she was doing something wrong to me. I realized all she did was for my good. I just cannot help it but to thank her for teaching me to be a better man. My uncle was a busy man and very quiet. His wife was in charge of making major decisions for the family. What she said in most cases made sense. I had to accept the new rules and circumstances; this was the road I had traveled. It was rocky but there I was at the time. One thing I was sure of was that good days were ahead and I had to follow through. The storm was heavy and the tunnel seemed too long; I still hope to see the sunlight. I wanted to walk this road regardless of the challenges. This was a tough life for an early teenager.

Life that is beyond human control is impossible to do anything about it. I was in another world, around people I still had to know. Sometimes, I felt like I was hit by a hurricane. I never knew then why it had to be that way, but it was happening to me. I was going through life's circumstances like many did.

I was too young for all of this. What have I done to deserve some of the ordeals in life? Life went on. I returned to school six months later. Thank God for his priceless intervention and to my uncle and his wife. To me, I felt time seemed wasted, not all was lost however.

School in Lofa

In school after a year was like being in heaven. I was gradually withstanding the test of time. The moment I had long waited for was here. I went to school almost every day and worked hard to do better in school among my classmates. For sure, this was my intention.

Life with my uncle was good. He was considered a wealthy man in his county. Our neighbors and strangers who visited the town admired us. Once more, I was in a life of comfort, but with attached conditions. This life brought memories of my parents. We had almost everything we needed to survive. Living with my uncle, we had enough food which I shared with my neighbors. The little money I got from Uncle and his wife, and other household goods I took from home, was used to help those in needs.

It hurt me to see poverty with my own eyes. Why were some so poor? Yet, they seemed happy. Life is not fair. Some were rich while many were poor. Poverty in Africa is different from poverty in the West. In Africa, those who are considered poor, some can be happy as long as there is peace. In the West, the story is different. Some farmers are wealthy in the West. In Africa, farmers sometimes cannot feed themselves, especially when there is national instability. Some barely feed their families, while farming on small scales. I felt something could be wrong. Why are some so wealthy and others poor? Is this injustice and inequality? However, there are poor and rich people in life. Helping each other is the best way to go about it. Sitting at the dinner table to eat, my heart was troubled. "We have so much to eat, why not the others? It was impossible to eat sometimes because of this guilt. I was not responsible for this problem. I was only a living witness. I was too young, and should be thinking about playing with friends and going to school. Why was I concerned about an issue I couldn't do anything about? That was the beginning of the awareness in my life. I came to know later that poverty is a worldwide problem, and that it has been around from the birth of humanity, from one generation to another. The struggle in every society has been, and continues to be a major problem with many suggestions to be answers.

Life with my aunt and my parents was long past, and gone, but the memories of those good and bad days are still remembered.

The struggle in uncle's family grew and had weighed on the family's progress. Uncle's status had a consequence; he was constantly under observation by some of his wife's family and friends. He was known to have had relationships with other women before he met his wife. Because of the number of people living in the house, too many things started to unfold. His wife concentrated on the business they had. He went to work and she had to supervise the family alone. This was too much for her. I admired her strength and the ability to conduct multiple tasks alone as a woman.

She is the kind of woman a man can rely on and hold on to, with God first. She was not educated woman, but very intelligent in all of her interactions with people she comes across in her everyday life. I was happy at times, but when there was tension, I was worried. "What is going on and what can I do? I asked. I got along with everyone in the family, but I still had yet to fully understand my surroundings. Uncle was away most of the day and came home in the evening. His wife had too much on her plate to handle. So I saw where her frustrations came from on some days.

My third younger brother was very quiet and easygoing. He spoke softly and hated any confrontation. I was strong, active and could defend myself when attacked by other boys. I hated confrontation back then as I do now. I was from the city and spoke English. All I wanted in Lofa was to make friends and to play. I was acquainted with the ways of city life that I wanted my new friends to know. I enjoyed listening to them telling me wonderful love stories, filled with affections, the hero and the bad guy. When you hear the stories, all you could think about is love. Your emotions just felt in the right place. When I used to be alone I kept thinking about those lovely stories.

I told the boys this: "I don't like to fight. I like making friends." The message resonated well; they were willing to be friends. We were cool; and we played together.

Constant complaints about me and one of my nephews by Uncle's wife took a toll in the house. The reason was we were out late hanging out with friends etc. This sort of uneasiness bothered them. Action was taken to prevent the family from falling apart. Two years later, we were sent to neighboring Sierra Leone to continue our education. By this time, I was in the 2,nd and going to the 3rd grade. I left Foya with one of uncle's daughters; she was older than all of us. This eased the tension and gave them the chance to look after our younger ones. But news of our departure brought sadness. I was leaving friends and family to go to an unknown land. It was a good decision but I was too young to comprehend what was taking place. They were preparing us for the future.

I had met a girl I was in love with in Lofa. It had been three to four months. It was hard telling her I was about to leave. I had no choice and could not prevent this trip from taking its course. I was sick for almost a week, but I had to go. My uncle reiterated his intention to take us, no matter what. The final straw had broken the camel's back.

On eve of our departure we were given almost everything we needed to take with us. We had money and the necessary things to use. We were going to a boarding school. There, I would learn how to grow up to be a decent person. Before we left, my cousins and other family members gave us hugs; we all shared those bitter tears many have shared when family members are departing to some faraway land.

My girlfriend could not let go of me. I visited her the night before we left. We were together all day and night. We were in hiding because our parents thought we were too young to do the boyfriend and girlfriend stuff. No one could question our love. It was love at first sight and I had no means of rejecting this love. However, I had to leave the next day. The journey was long and hard. Some of us took sick, but we made it.

A Student in Bo District

The people in the village of Bumpeh were very friendly, and they willingly accepted us. This was a new life among the Mende people of Sierra Leone. Everything was different; including the language. I was growing up, learning how to speak English and my native language.

In Sierra Leone, I tried to speak Mende; I learned how to speak English using the British accent. This was interesting for me. I loved it at first, but as soon as classes were in progress I also learned what it was like to be a part of a boarding school; it was like a military base with real duties and punishment. What I learned from that campus prepared me to be strong and to deal with some of the challenges in life. What I also learned helped me deal with some of life most troubling issues that came my way.

Those techniques learned on the Bumpeh campus broadened my survivor skills to learn how to accept my condition and to work towards finding solutions. We were trained to be hard working and to become decent people in our community. I was quickly initiated into the system and became very happy with my new friends.

Having experienced these predicaments without fully understanding why, I was learning the true meaning of life. The only thing I knew was to cope with the unpleasant realities at the time.

In Sierra Leone, I forgot about my past for a while, I had friends to play with most of the time, which was what I needed. There was no need for me to worry about food or taking care of myself. The food and everything were different and the language sounded different. My life was on campus without my parents, was on my mind. The psychological and physical damage will last for a long time and this loss made me appreciate life and to accept the things I cannot change. No one can fill that gap. Mothers are very special.

In a faraway land this intense feeling of loneliness and the longing to be with my mother reminded me of what it meant to be loved and to be cared for. I still remember the hugs, the kisses, and those tender hands I felt when I was with her. Tears became my friend and pain my companion. These were the emotional struggles; I had to learn how to cope with. When I am attacked by those sad moments, I only find a quiet place, especially in such a melancholy mood. Thinking and talking to myself, at the same time asking God to help me make sense of my life in the world with tears. I wanted some comfort to come from somewhere, but where. I was alone and didn't want to expose my feelings to friends and strangers around me; they didn't understand what I was really experiencing. Explaining to them would cause me additional pain and emotional breakdown.

I was like a small man on the battlefield fighting alone to defeat the enemy. I had no other way of retreating from the battlefield. I had to trust God to win this war. This was a war not against anyone, but a war with me and the circumstances in life that kept beating against my family. I started a race but I had no clue how it would end. The race seemed too long for me. However, I had to keep running. That is what I had to do. It felt, I was racing alone, but were these invincible forces running the race with me. How can you win a race with competitors you sometimes cannot see? God had to be my coach, the captain, as well as my comforter. These were the forces of good and evil. I believed I had God on my side and the good angels who guided my footsteps. This had to be the blessing from above. In those heart-breaking moments, I wanted to be left alone. Only God knew what was going through my mind. The agony of not being with my parents connected with the complicated life style I had found myself in. All seemed too much to bear or take. The burden was too heavy for me to carry alone. I needed some supernatural powers to help me at this time. Everywhere I turned for help, brought me back to the truth. I had to face the realities, happening at the time, and to wait on God's appointed time.

During my stay in Bumpeh, Sierra Leone, life took a drastic turn that affected my schooling there. The short happiness had turned into one of tragic episode. Two and half years had passed and we had gotten adjusted, but not too comfortable with the life of campus. Nothing we could do about it. For my niece, she was a female and her life was different from the boys. My younger brother who was so brilliant fell sick with diabetes, and was taken to one of the best hospitals in Bo district, Sierra Leone, West Africa. The head of the school could not think of anyone to be with him but me. I was still in school and was about to start my final exams that year. We were excited to go back in Liberia. Everything changed not for the good but for the worst. I was hit once more by forces that were beyond my control. As I watched my brother lying helplessly I prayed, asking God to please save his life, "Was there anything I could do, Father?" I asked.

My mother was away. I cried deep down from the bottom of my heart. I felt we were losing him. He tried many times to remain strong but was over taken by the sickness we knew nothing about. It was another terrible blow to the family. In the hospital his sickness moved from bad to worst. The doctors observed he was going to die. They requested the school board to send for Uncle my brother home. I had faith I hoped he would live to see more years. My wish was a primitive one. I was not matured enough to understand something was about to happen. The answer was simple. The doctors discharged him and asked he be taken home where he could die peacefully. He was very young. Why had death taken him away at such age? I had little experience. I had to leave to take my finals. I left but a paid person replaced me to look after him.

My uncle came on time upon knowledge of the news of my dying brother; a sense of relief came over me that they had come for him. Two weeks later I received news of his death. I was broken by the news. My world crumbled once again. "Marcus," as he was affectionately called, was the only one among my brothers who was with me in Foya and on campus in Sierra Leone. The next thing that came to my mind was how mother would react to the death of the son she had not seen for years. The smell of death had hit my family again. Buried in my absence, I wanted to see him for the last time to pay my respect or to say good-bye. "Heaven," I called for answers.

Like me, many have felt the pain of death of a loved one. I shared their bitter tears and I couldn't share them anymore. Friends and schoolmates tried to console me. I needed sometime to accept the fact that brother was dead and gone, until we meet again someday in heaven. I did not have the power to undo what had occurred. The only thing left was to endure this horrible time in my life. I had to put everything behind me and to move on with my life. His death had left a scar on my mind that could not be erased. I had to take the memories with me for the rest of my life. I needed a change somewhere to get over his death. I couldn't continue to attend school in Sierra Leone, knowing very well that part of me was gone. I felt completely out of order and almost lost all focus for that semester in school. That is how things ended for me in Sierra Leone.

I was on the road again. Once more I left friends behind those friends who meant everything to me. The playing and the fun days were over for a while. My plan was to leave and return to Lofa. Upon hearing my plan, my campus girlfriend didn't want to lose me, nor let me go. She was deeply in love. She was by my side throughout this unforgettable trend in life. She did ask an emotional question I had no answer for. "Are you leaving me here?" This question took my breath away. We became so close that it seemed impossible to separate us. We cried together and hugged each other. This moment was like being out of this world.

I felt lost in her arms. We were in another world of our own. Silence was our answer in this agony moment of truth. No one could comfort the other. Only tears kept running down our faces. We were bonded by love and sorrows at the same time. We just could not afford to leave each other. We had some good times making love on the green grass. Even in the river we went to take our bath. Everything that transpired between us was memories that were kept for remembrance.

In those good and bad days, I kept in my heart for years ahead of me. I do at times; reflect on those bitters sweet childhood days. Finally, I left her in tears. That was my life at that time. As long as we live in a world that is unpredictable, we can expect anything.

My uncle and his wife came back at the end of the semester. I gathered my things to depart Sierra Leone for Liberia. We prepared for our departure. My friends and my girlfriend were there to support me as I departure. I looked them in the eyes and found out they were sad. We gathered together, and encouraged ourselves with words we couldn't speak out. Everything in my midst seemed lost and helpless. I had wished and hoped for nothing at all. Life I thought was an enemy and I had no logical way to get out of it. The driver was ready to leave; I did not want to leave her in tears. These were the people I cherished most at this time. I was leaving them in this manner? They were there for me throughout my stay in Sierra Leone. The times we spent together in school and during lunch and dinner, became things of the past. Everything was falling apart. They were true friends I held dearly in my heart. I loved them and had wished I could spend my lifetime with them. What I did not realize at first was that people come and go. "Life can be sad sometimes," I said to myself. We hugged each other, but were unable to say goodbye. Like it is being said, "there are times in life when everyman has to face the truth." I was facing mine. I was too young and immature to deal with the unforeseen circumstances that were taken place.

In Lofa, life was different than what it was back in the days when I was there with my uncle's family. I was dealing with the loss of my brother and premature departure from school. My friends on campus were family I knew and departing from them was like losing the world and life. I felt lonely and was depressed. The only thing I could think of was to leave Lofa and that was part of the solution to my problems. I felt I had too much on my hand to handle and needed some rest for a moment. Those who knew me observed something was wrong. Neighbors stopped by, visited for a while, and were gone.

Those friends I knew in Lofa came around to wish me well. Those happy moments, if there were any, were gone for a while. Hopeless over the loss of a brother and worry about mother were my main concern. My priorities were very particular. I had principles when dealing with my age group. My life had changed entirely. Even my uncle and his wife saw these changes. I worked fully with her and uncle in the most respectable manner. I was different in my new way of doing things. I was forced to adapt to my new ways of life. I could not depart from it. The changes were a part of life.

Thanks to my good parents, and the teachers I met in Sierra Leone; they gave me the relevant tools I needed to live as a decent person. One thing I was not yet aware of was that the ladder was still long to climb. I had to trust God to be strong and ready to face any event. In my heart I became a person needing strength to go through life on a day to day basis. Fear was gone because the troubles were many. However, all seemed just the beginning. I forgot some of the things that took place during these difficult time and period. On the other hand, having lost my brother in an unexpected way, affected my strength as a teenager. I felt, sometimes completely worthless. Life didn't make much sense at the time. The desert was the best place to be, so I thought. There, maybe, I would have some peace. No one at the time could bring me the peace I desired in life. Hope was all I needed. The only thing I contemplated on was that anything could happen at any time. "Why should I worry anymore," I told myself. Life, as I thought was not in my favor. I was like an outcast who no one cares about. I prayed that the following day would be one day at a time.

My uncle and his wife made the final decision for my departure to Monrovia. I welcomed their plan. They did their best but as a teen,

I saw things differently, added by the loss of my brother I felt sad. He understood me better. My uncle and his wife were too busy with family, work, and business to fill the gap left behind by my parents. They did their best to help me through the process. Maybe a change in location was eminent or necessary for me. I needed some space in life. We were only children and we all needed parental monitoring and supervision. We were too many to get the attention at once at home.

Before brother's death, my mother, together with her new husband once passed through Lofa to visit Guinea, where his family came from. Mother's new husband, I thought, was the worst person I ever met in my life. By this time, they had three children. I knew only one of them. In Guinea, my mother found herself caught between "the devil and the deep blue sea." She was advised by members of the church she attended that her visit to Guinea with my little sister would bring some serious setback for her. Did my mother ignore this warning from the church?

She was in love with this man. The only problem was his addiction to alcohol. He was almost incapable of responsibility; it made life more stressful. But as the saying goes sometimes, "love is blind." I accepted this fact later on my journey in life, but that too would change. As a child, I didn't know how to deal with the situation. All I thought was that we were her children and we were the ones she had after my dad's death. As I grew older, I realize we all make mistakes. I thought she could protect us from a stranger who seemed unable to function well because of his addiction to alcohol at the time. We were too young to deal with our step-dad's addiction problem. The way he treated us, at times made us sad and being in his mist when he was drunk was something hard to handle.

On that visit to Guinea, my little sister took sick and within matter of days, was in a critical condition. In few weeks she was pronounced dead. Had the warning made by the church came to pass? We were told my sister died by witchcraft, according to information that circulated around town. I had no way to justify this information. Wherever they went through the Town, those they came across had something to say about sister's beauty. She had long curly hair. My sister's hair had to be cut to prevent it from growing too long. This was one of the most difficult times for my mother.

She had five boys with my dad, no girls. She was desperate for one. When she finally met my step-dad, she prayed and God answered her prayer.

The news of my brother's death still awaited her. It took her breath away and left her almost helpless. She lost all sense of being and sorrow she lived with for years to come. Nothing anyone could offer as a gift in exchange for her loss. The Creator was the only one who eased her pain. Two of her kids were dead. Solitude was the best thing she wanted. However, she had to move on with life while living with the memories.

After sister's burial in Guinea my mother and step dad returned to Foya, Liberia. I lived here with uncle and his wife. Once more, I was privileged to meet and see mother after few years. I was relieved. I saw the woman who gave me birth, once more. We were happy and sad at the same time when we met in Foya. I was covered with blanket of a mother's love once again. This love was what I had dreamed. Material things are good but the absence of a mother's love, nothing can replace it. Having had all these terrible experiences, mother decided to take a giant step. She was tired of being away from her family. She blamed herself for some the family's setbacks. No matter what went wrong, we are her children. She finally decided to bring the remaining children back.

We spent the night in the same room and we had some lengthy discussions. That was progress. I began to learn my position in life with my reunion with mother. I saw instantly what the family went through. My mother spent two to three weeks in Foya; mother gathered her belongings from the Town. She agreed go to Monrovia where it all started. Her return was significant for the families.

In Monrovia

My older brother was already in Monrovia with one of my uncles. I was the only one in Lofa to join the rest of the family in Monrovia. I was happy. Even though I had some doubts about reunion, I took the risk. Finally, I made it to Monrovia. Life was different now and the people I left behind have either gone to different places or dead. Some of the friends I had and knew were gone. Some of the few I left behind had grown up in age. I grew a little taller myself. My environment had changed a great deal. New houses were under construction and we had new neighbors as well.

The friends I left behind were very happy to see me once again. We laughed and played and talked about my experiences abroad. I was put in charge of my dad's house. Mother later came with my younger brothers from Grand Bassa County, south east of Liberia, where she lived with her new husband. It was a day of celebration! There was no party but the reunion meant everything to us in the world. This was our wish and dream. We loved and cared for each other. We were never selfish to one another. That was what our parents taught us and that's what we had as part of our lives. We loved our friends and neighbors. My mother told us to be kind towards them. We did just that. I was now in the seventh grade and was about to start school again. We had started new life again after all we went through. We knew we needed each other at this time. We had to survive and return to school at the same time. Mother had little money and wanted to establish her business in Monrovia. We had to feed, wear clothe and attend school. It was impossible. Two of my brothers were very young and did not understand the purpose of education or its importance. So, I was the first to start school again.

I was blessed to receive assistance from the church where our dad served as deacon. This good gesture could help with some of the financial burden on the family that was trying to lift itself up before the war. Mother returned to the market every day, I left early morning to catch the bus to school. When school was over for the day I took my brothers home and watched them as I cooked for the house. I did laundry, cleaned up and represented the family at meetings in the community. I did things I was not ready for. I read all business letters, especially electric and water bills. Responsibilities made a man out of me. I was focused and listened very carefully to details and instructions. My neighbors mentioned I would be the man who would step in my dad's shoes to support the family. In my culture, there is a saying that, "There is no little man." The advice I received kept me awake. I missed lot of things and activities. I could not play or hangout like most of my friends.

My education and my family's obligations were priorities on my list. I was growing up, being a strong person in Christ, one who others could depend on. I loved doing things to make others happy. Being kind to others was my confidence. It was worth doing things that brought smile to someone.

I loved my mother very much and we were very close too. We were best friends. We worked with each other peacefully. Mother always advised me to stay away from the girls, but they kept finding me no matter what.

After returning to Monrovia, Mother was surprised to see the changes in my attitude. She loved asking questions. "What really took place on that campus?" We were disciplined to become good people to impact our various societies. They did not spare the rod, meaning, our teachers and deans used the Cane whenever we misbehaved. She laughed and made a comment on how she used the Cane herself to discipline us when we were bad kids. It was very nice of them. "You are now good in doing so many things, especially at home and when dealing with people," she said. She was very proud and happy that I had become the person she had wished all her lifetime for me. Despite all of these positive signs, more was needed for my own good. Time was the only thing to determine what was ahead of the family. I had to remain dedicated to doing the right thing, to reach the heights I dreamed many years ago. My mother was very certain the future was to be fruitful for me. She always wished me her blessing for obeying her commands and thanked God for all we had gone through and the circumstances we were dealing with.

This was a good mother, hoping that her children have a brighter future. At night, while sleeping, I heard my mother praying in the middle of the night when everyone was at sleep, asking God to restore happiness once more to our family. She shared those heart-breaking tears. She was still a widow with no one to really help her but God. She had left my step father because things were out of order. I will never forget that in my entire existence. I had every reason to pursue education despite the difficulties. I saw what my mother

47

went through growing up. Her happy days were few, but her life was compounded by grieve and life's tribulations. Life went on as she continued to trust the Lord for peace. Everything that happened in my family awakened me to be stronger. I wondered and searched for my purpose here on this earth. Like me, many are going through the same to discover their mission in this world. Some find the answers but many are still trying to do so.

I needed time to reintegrate in Liberia. The city I left for few years looked different in my eyes. Liberians, who are known to be very lean- back, used most of their spare time by sitting either in front or at the back of their porches at home with family or friends drinking their favorite drink, "beer." If they were working after work, they were in the habit of making a stop at one of the local bars of their choice of drinking and having fun while hanging out with friends.

Those visiting the same bars were familiar with each other and could share drinks. As long as you were a member of a particular night club and was known by other friends you didn't have to carry money all the time to get a drink. The bar's customers would provide for those who were broke. To me, this was a good life and it also represented unity among the people. Some were sitting on their balcony and others relaxing.

Parents were warning their teenagers not to mess with alcohol. One would be punished when caught in the act and was spotted by the older guys in the family. Drinking liquor was mostly associated with few people in their thirties and above. It was something almost every young person in my country respected. Some went undercover to drink a little just to get a taste of what alcohol was like. This was before the Liberian Civil War.

Observing what was happening in the city, I said to myself, "I like the city and the way my people were mingling with each other." Liberians were known to be very kind. I think this is a good way for people to get along. Peace, love, and the kindness we enjoyed were to come to an end in the wake of the war. Life started to improve again but the good times did not last long.

The unexpected civil war was in the making. The brutal war would plunge the entire nation into chaos and everything it came into contact with, could perish. Some of us who were blessed to live after the war have to tell the story. Some fighters on both sides of the war were not informed of the true motives of the war. We did not know what to expect at that moment during the fighting.

Average people could be the victims of every conflict. Were we paying the price for the errors we made as a nation? Is this was the reason we, the young generation was deceived in the war, and some used as fighters? Some were forced to participate in the killings. The most disturbing pictures of the war were right in our faces. Like many war torn countries around the world, many, especially have been in Africa. The continent which civic unrest has affected the lives of millions, to the least form of human indignity, could continue if nothing much is done.

Civil wars, power struggles, corruption and poverty have rendered Africa further troubled.

Liberians waited eagerly for help from other nations around the world. The battle became bloodier; some felt abandoned as a people. About 300,000 to 500,000 Liberians died. We had the opportunity to adopt peace through dialogue but it was already too late. Violence became the way out of conflict. Liberians also died in poor countries in Africa. Some died from disease, poverty, starvation, poor health, discrimination, tribal attacks. Other reasons like false allegations and unfair trials landed many in prison mostly in developing countries, in Africa. As a result some were never seen or heard of up to this day. Some died of frustration because they felt or thought they had lost everything they had in life. We needed help urgently but what some of us didn't understand was how other governments reacted to conflicts. I realized that intervention forces that headed to troubled countries took time, and most of all, resources. This could make it almost impossible to get help quickly and prevent human casualties in crisis countries. No matter what the situation was like for us, our appreciation for countries which came to our help will never be forgotten. Those who risked and lost their lives to save us will be remembered as our heroes.

My appreciation goes to those who took their time to pass knowledge to some of us. I was privileged to attend school in other countries while the war was going on in Liberia. To all my professors and instructors at home and abroad, you guys are the heroes.

As fighting continued in Liberia we were left to die at the mercy of combatants. We were held under barrier of the gun. Many people died in the process. As I sat confined in my room in Monrovia, I thought and prayed for an end to the civil war. I had wished and hoped for life to return to normal once again. We were separated by war and there was no hope of finding anyone alive; only the grace of God was our hope. Bullets fled in every direction. One thing that remained on mind was corpses in the street. Civilians helped to bury dead bodies, some of which had decayed. Children held guns that were bigger. Prominent opposition leaders became the focus of warring factions in the conflict.

When rebels completely took over the city, I was arrested along with some neighbors and the only option we were left with was to join the fighting. This was a tough decision to make. We were pressured by rebels. Some gave in. I had nothing to do with fighting and my family warned us not to participate.

If my decision was going to cost me my life, so be it, I reminded myself. The Lord was on my side. Some of us were imprisoned and went without food for days. Some of us were willing to make any sacrifice than to take up arms against fellow Liberians. What was the reason we had turned against ourselves? I didn't know how to interpret the situation on ground at the time. Many times we were confused, waiting to find our next hiding place.

Finding food was a major problem. Streets were no longer safe. The war that started at the Liberian and Ivory Coast borders our government claimed was under control was a lie. A whole nation was under observation around the world. Like Rwanda, Sierra Leone and Sudan, to name a few, the world was watching us while we awaited some foreign intervention. But to intervene in another country's crisis requires careful assessment before the deployment of troops.

The West African Peacekeeping Force, (ECOMOG) headed by Nigeria and fully supported by the international community, came to our aid. Liberians will never forget the sacrifices made by Nigeria and ECOMOG; but the sad event we incurred, added to the massacre of a nation that was drowning. Looting was taken place on both sides. Some civilians also took part in this process.

There was lack of food in the city. I had to leave home to find food for my brother, and those who sought refuge at our house. It was a risk; I had to put my life on the line. I knew I was leaving to find food, not material things. I would make it home alive. Life or death was the choice anyone going out had to make. I would rather search for food than to die of starvation. I acted brave not because I wanted to but we needed food to survive, even if there was an ongoing serious fighting between rebels and government troops. On several occasions, I was lucky I brought food home. Some thought it was too risky to go out in search of food. I returned home unharmed because God was on my side. I came home with some food for the family. Some family members and friends decided to put their fears behind; they joined me in the search for more food.

As I said earlier, my mother, before the civil war, was with her second husband, with two of my youngest brothers and three other kids she had with this man. She had been away for almost three years and now the fighting was raging in the city. I worried whether I would ever have the chance to see her again. We have started life new and very fresh again after all that we had to put up with as a family. We knew that we needed each other during those difficult times. But starting life without one of us having a job was another setback. I was the second child for my mother and my older brother was almost out of high school and still living with my one of my uncles. We needed to survive and to attend school at the same time.

I love my mother very well and we were very close too. We were best friends. We worked with each other very gently and peacefully. My mother always advised me to stay away from the girls but they kept finding me no matter what. As a student, I worked hard and attended school regularly. I believed some blessings were good were along the way.

After resettling in Monrovia my mother was very surprised to see the changes in my attitude, since I left my country for Sierra Leone to attend school. My mother loved asking questions. She asked, "What really took place on that campus?" My response was; we were disciplined to become nice people, to impact our various societies. Also, they did not spare the rod, meaning our teachers and the deans used the cane whenever we misbehaved." She laughed and made a comment on how she used the cane to discipline us when we were bad kids. She also said "it was very nice of them. You are now good in doing so many things, especially at home and when dealing with people." She was very proud and happy that I was becoming the person she had wished all her lifetime for me to be.

These positive attributes in me needed to be accomplished. Time was the only thing that would determine what lay ahead of the family. I had to remain dedicated to what I was doing in order for me to reach the height I had dreamed of many years ago. My mother was very certain that the future had to be fruitful for me. She always wished me her blessing for obeying her commands and she always thanked God for all that we had gone through, and for all the circumstances that we had yet to deal with.

This was a good mother hoping that her children would have a brighter future. At night while sleeping, I would hear my mother praying in the middle of the night when everyone was at sleep, "asking God to restore happiness once more to our family." She would share those heart-breaking tears. She was a widow with no one to really turn to for help, but God alone. I will never forget that in my entire existence. I had all reasons to pursue education despite the difficulties involved.

I have seen what my mother went through while growing up. Everything that had happened in my family had awakened me to be strong. However, my dream still had to be fulfilled. I was still wondering and searching for my purpose of being on this earth. Like me, many are going through the same process to discover what their missions in world have to be. Some will find answers while others still keep on searching.

Since my arrival from Sierra Leone and back in Liberia, I needed time to reintegrate into the most unique Liberian culture I had known. A lot has changed while I was out of the country for almost five years. The city was very lively and people seemed to be having so much fun. Observing what was happening in the city, I said to myself "I like the city and the way my people were mingling with each other."

Liberians were known to be very kind in nature. I was brought up in such environment and this was just a way of life. I think this was a better way for people to get along. Life was tough at first, but things started to improve gradually. Once again I started having fun with friends and girls were coming around as well. Life was good again. However, the good times were not to last long.

Having spent three years in the capital city of Liberia, Monrovia, life was getting better for my family after all the hard times we went through. One thing most of us never expected was in the making. The brutal war would plunge the entire nation into chaos and every-thing it came in contact with, perished. For some of us who would be blessed to live after the war we have to tell the story.

LT. Romeo Dallaire, the commander for UN Peacekeeping Force in Rwanda, in his book on Rwanda, "Shake Hands with the Devil," he asked this question; "Who are we?" For some of us, selflessness could be a way of life. I can safely assume that Liberians will never repeat such conflict in our history. They learned their lessons.

It had been four months since the civil war started. We were run-ning out of food fast. I was worried and had grown thin. My body was declining rapidly and I had to do something to keep me alive. We had to leave the city, somewhere to find food, provided we survive among the fighters. My neighbors were faced with the same decision. We call for an emergency meeting to find solution to our hunger crisis. My plan was to get out of the city to the interior. It was not easy to convince the people to leave the city. We had to make quick decision because time was running out. Rampant killings were everywhere. Almost everyone was starving. Only rebels and government troops had food–this was a dangerous situation for us.

The journeying to reach Lofa on foot took about a month's walk. There was no hope of finding food along the way except when we were lucky. Many people were leaving the city. It was a mass exodus and a forceful one. Some reached their homes in the interior but others did not. They were either killed by rebels or by government troops. Many perished because there was no food for them to survive the trip. It was sad to watch what was unfolding. This was the reality we were seeing and experiencing. The fighting left people confused with no sense of direction.

Some kind of conclusion was reached after our meeting to depart the city for the interior. It was the chance we thought made sense. Some wanted to stay because they weren't too sure where they were going; safe drinking water had been tinted. Finally, we gathered everything we could take with us for our departure.

I took few clothes and the little money I had. For my older brother, he wasn't prepared to leave, but said; he needed to prepare his mind. His idea made some sense. I tried to convince him to think about it. We insisted he make up his mind soon. He decided he was leaving some of his clothes from one of our uncle's place. I had no power to stop him because he was my senior brother. I was in approval of that decision he made.

Bullets were flying everywhere and many people were dying from stray bullets. There came a problem of identification of the enemies and friends. The rebels dressed just like civilians, which meant that, anyone could be wrongly accused by government troops for wrong identity. The rebels too were concerned that spies from government troops were posing as civilians. This was a deadly situation. No one knew for sure if they would live to see another day. We were now trapped between rebels and government soldiers.

Brother decided he was prepared to leave. I was concerned about letting him leave my presence. He left to go pack his clothes. I never knew he was saying, good bye. That was the last day I saw my brother. He became a victim of a war that was killing innocent people. We heard he was killed. No one knows the truth surrounding his disappearance and his sudden death. His hand I held that day was my last touch. Why did I let go of that hand? I could not be blamed. It was hard to believe or accept that another innocent victim was dead.

He was not one of the fighters, so why was he killed, and by whom? Only God knows. But in every conflict, the innocence could be the prey. I kept thinking about mother and how she would take the news. This time, it was her oldest son, killed in a deadly civil war. Who were responsible for this brutal war?

The entire country was sunk in total lawlessness. I waited so long, hoping that brother would return so we could leave the city for the interior together. Was he killed on his way to uncle's house? I felt and knew something went wrong, but I didn't want to admit to the fact he was dead. It was something no one could easily accept. The trip to Lofa was delayed because we were waiting on brother's return. The neighbors and I waited. There was no trace of my brother. I lost all hope and felt hopeless. Everything inside of me faded like a shutdown machine. I was lost in my own world. I had no answer for the things that were happening around me. My brother who was close to me was gone forever. He was my best friend. We went almost everywhere together. I was lonely and had only God to trust. I needed the strength to cope with this huge loss in my life. It was silent a dilemma. I was hurt and sad. I felt I was not treated fairly by life. Everything was over and there was nothing left for me to lose, I thought. I was ready and fully willing to travel to Lofa. What the consequences were, I did not want to think about it anymore. After all, my life was no better than a young child soldier fighting and dying every single day in the war. So if that was the case I too was no better. I left everything in the hands of God. What was to be, had to take place? I could not make any changes to what was already happening. That was the way life was for the time being. I had to live through it till the end of the war if I would live to see the end.

All the pain I felt and witnessed others went through during the civil war brought changes in my life. I lost two of my best friends and one of my uncles as a result of the civil war. The civil war had opened my eyes to the cruelty and selfishness of this world. What our eyes were revealed to is something many will never forget. As I walked the streets of Monrovia, I was terrified by some of the horrific scenery some people were killed. I saw someone dying slowly and struggling to take his last breath. His killers used a knife to open his stomach while his intestines dropped on the floor, and he dragged himself just to live. I saw he was really in pain. There was no one to lend a helping hand. He died slowly. "Is there any reason why he had to die in such a manner?" I asked myself. I tried to make sense of the situation, but I was young.

On another occasion, I witnessed another gruesome scene where a man was beheaded from the back of his neck, but his killers didn't cut his head off completely. They left him to die in a cruel way. He was there trying to lift his neck, but only a piece of his head laid hanging on his left shoulder. He was dragging on his neck just to live. The brutal way in which some were murdered, according to some people I met during the war, was revenge taking by their killers. How true was the reason for such killing I had no answer? I could not tell who was offering a true version of the story. What can one expect when lawlessness had taken over? I had to calm down for a moment to ask myself a question: Is there any love in this world. If so, where was it gone?"

Every time I went in the house of God, the preacher emphasized the importance love. Is love real? If this is true, why then do we hurt each other in many vile ways? And why do we have to take guns against each other? I felt I was deceived and that there was no love in the world. Now I know love is real. God's love is the best.

Recollection of massacre of innocent men, women and children is still fresh on the minds of those of us who witnessed the civil war.

It is good to have money, but anything one could desire in life, like material possessions meant nothing at all at this time. Those caught in the civil war, prayed to live and to see another day. Memories of what I saw kept haunting my mind regularly. "What a world. I reminded myself? Why was I born in the first place? Why were we going through all this battle just to cope with life and understand what it really meant especially for children"?

I wanted to be in school, or spending time with my parents and friends. No, instead, I was praying to God to save me and to preserve my life against forces of evil, the evil that had descended on our nation. I found myself in a quandary position. During those cat-astrophic moments, no one answered my questions. I was confused, and somehow abandoned. I wished I was in the desert to stay away from the fighting. Life in the wilderness I guess was the perfect place to be. Life among some people and friends, but were now fighting themselves seemed, to be the last place for humans to live and sur-vive. It was like hell on earth. Was this the hell I was told about many years as a child? At this point, we didn't know who to trust. Only God one could trust.

During the war, best friends betrayed each other for money, mate-rial things or properties. Brothers and sisters took up against the other. Human beings had no value anymore in the midst disorder. No one was held accountable for the atrocities that were committed by warring factions and government troops who were supposed to protect us. The masters were those in arms. The question of right or wrong was no more. Fighters took the law into their own hands and did anything they wanted. This was not the Liberia many were born and raised in. Liberians were helpless in their own country. As I walked the streets of Monrovia I saw many asked in Monrovia asked as to where they were going. Shootings were heard everywhere in Monrovia. Indiscriminate killings were common everywhere. No life was guaranteed another day. Every one's life depended on the grace and mercy of God. The challenges for Liberians were too much.

Child, mother, father or even any living creature was vulnerable. There was complete breakdown of law and order. We were huddled like sardines. One could be killed for anything or any reason. The blood of the innocent cried out to God for help. The only opportunity some waited for was to get out of Monrovia or out of the country. It was too late for some to do anything, or coordinate any plan to get out of the country. All many wished for was for the civil war to come to an end for us to live once more as people, putting the past behind.

My uncle and his family had left for the interior after they failed to persuade me to leave the city at once and follow them to the borders between Liberia and Sierra Leone. I loved Monrovia and was used to being a city boy. I regretted my stubbornness. I was now in limbo. My life was in jeopardy because I couldn't think of the journey on foot to Lofa. I paid a severe price for ignoring my uncle's warning.

August 3, 1990, is the date and month I will always remember because it was the time I finally departed Monrovia. I was not the only one who left on that day and with me were some of my neighbors who agreed to travel with us to Lofa. This adventure was risky because our decision came late. We knew that this late decision was a gamble for life or death. This was the price anyone willing to flee the fighting could pay for late decision. It was a difficult decision to choose between comfort and adventure.

Traveling by foot to other parts of Liberia during the war was at this point was like suicide. We were aware that there was shortage of food, water, and the absence of a safe journey. Flying bullets could reach anyone on that journey, and could end his or her live. This was the kind of experience no one could imagine going through for most of the time during the civil war. Many people suffered because of the misguided direction. Many Liberians, for some reasons or the other, blamed themselves for taking side early in a misguided war.

The combatants in the civil war, some were not intelligent; they unwisely turned their weapons on helpless and defenseless Liberians. A child soldier who killed civilians only added to the tragedy. Some were forcefully recruited to fight for the various warring factions. They were deceived and falsely promised paradise on earth. Meaning, the warlords promised to reward them upon victory at the end of the war. Rebel commanders eliminated many of them to avoid fulfilling the promises they could not keep, especially those who felt threatened by the intelligence of some of their young fighters. Rebels' followers chose aggression over simple persuasion skill. It was the most catastrophic mistake.

The fact that some Liberians helped to mislead President Samuel Doe, whose lust for power, never had the nerve to put his nation first was an added blunder to the whole fiasco in the Liberian dilemma. Some of us never knew what the consequences of our misleading involvement in the conflict would be.

Some politicians mostly focused on their political agendas- getting power by any means necessary. We could have left room in reaching some realistic dialogue. Liberians had to pay a price for the errors some made. Those who died were lying in the streets with flies all over them, and their decaying bodies like animals killed and left to get rot. It was sad as Liberians bled during the war.

It was a shame to watch what was taken place. Perhaps some regretted their actions. Liberians will never forget that the civil uprising was the most damaging and aggressive conflict in history. For those of us who survived the civil war, we are forced to be the ones to explain the truth of what we witnessed. Those who took part in the civil war, nor we who had nothing to do with the fighting, should put aside our differences and live together as brothers and sisters. Peace I believe makes more sense than looking for means to revenge.

I always felt obligated to write or narrate to the world and my readers about my childhood, and the bitter experiences during the civil war. I have, on many times; turned away from writing what many Liberians like me went through to survive the war, but my body, mind, spirit, kept reminding me I have to sit down to share our troubled experiences. For those who died, we owe them this much. That is, to write and inform the world and the present generation the impact the war had on the people of Liberia. Many of those who died were the sons and daughters of ordinary Liberian families and the innocent. Why the story will be told from many fronts, we should do our best to let go of the past to embrace a new era in our history. According to an eye witness account, a former combatant I met during the civil war said, some children were in school when the rebels surrendered our towns, capturing students, and forcing them to fight and to make sure children join in the fighting. The rebels executed some of the children in front of us to convince us we too had no option as well. If we refuse, that was the way we too were going to be executed.

The saddest picture left behind is the thousands of widows and children.

Was there any way out for those children? We created some of the deadliest killers in the conflict. A child solider did not have the chance to judge what they were told to do. Warlords also drugged them to carry out their killings. Under such influence, it was difficult for them to think straightly. The only thing those young killers wanted to do was to kill and glorify in the blood of their victims. Innocent people had to die for this senseless reason. Lack of good or sound judgment to separate the innocent people from the fighters was the saddest part.

On my journey to Lofa with the shortage of food except contaminated water, it was dangerous to our health. Some had no choice, but to drink any water just to survive and continue the journey. Spending days and nights on the way without proper sleep was draining to one's health.

I was on a journey with people thrice my age and much stronger. They kept pushing me to do my best and keep walking even when so tired. I almost gave up; my feet were swollen and could not keep using them. I had no choice. I knew and trusted these people. If anything had happened to me they would be the ones to break the silence to my family.

I was concerned about my mother, who was also worried for her children. One thing she had no knowledge of was that my senior brother was dead or missing. It was so hard for me to depart the city without my brother. Even my feet were heavy under me. It was true he was resting in peace with God in Heaven. This was the only song I heard in my ears. Someday I believe' we may uncover the truth about his death. I wish some day we will meet in heaven. We prayed his soul rest in peace and the innocents killed in the civil war.

Traveling without hope of finding food was just too stressful and crazy. We kept on with the journey. I was renewed from the encouragement of the people I was traveling with. One did not want to stay behind and get killed by unsympathetic fighters. That was our source of strength. I kept praying to God to renew my energy so I could hold on. I was weak and had lost a lot of weight. No one could easily recognize me because of my body condition and appearance.

The people in the towns and villages along the way were fearful of both rebels and government troops. Some abandoned their towns and villages. The villagers, some also hide their food because they wanted to survive on the little they had. They also had another issue of trust as well. They wished they could provide little food for travelers, but had fears of being betrayed.

This whole strategy was to prevent intruders from breaking through their self-defense. This made the journey even more devastating and unpredictable. The few clothes I took with me became too heavy to carry. I lost a lot of weight; I was starving and could no longer continue to carry them. My life and survival was more important than clothes. So my final decision was to let go some of the clothes. I gave some of my clothes to villagers we met along the way. They were very appreciative. I was pleased about their appreciation. This was not something strange to me. I was brought up and taught to always share with those in need when in the position to do so. "Be your brothers keepers." At times, when I thought of giving up hope for something I dearly needed, someone from nowhere stretched his or her kind hand.

The journey was hectic and full of confusion as well. There were arguments among travelers about finding the right direction traveling to Lofa. Rain, sunshine, cold, thirst, and the heat, were natural problems we had to face. The hills were very long and required long walking before completing them. We slept in bushes and sometimes in open areas because the towns were either far from our reach, or, we were not too sure how close we were to a town or village.

Mosquitoes became our worst enemies on the journey. No one complained that they had malaria because we were in the battle between life and death. As a Liberian I knew these deadly enemies.

When approaching some towns' or villages at times we were informed about fighting between the government troops and the rebels. Those who brought this information eventually fled the area to live to see another day and with such information, we wasted no time in changing our routes. We had to jump in the bushes to hide from all sides in the fighting because we could not tell readily which side was on our side.

The journey was a do or die battle for those of us who chose to take the risk. Along the way, there were times when we were stopped by rebels and interrogated about the tribes we belonged to. Some managed to get away by lying they were members from another tribe. In my opinion, the whole issue of tribal hatred was senseless. People from all tribes within the country, some were killed. Every tribal member suffered, or was one way or the order affected by the war. Many never reached their families in the interior alive because they were falsely accused.

According to the rebels, the targeted tribes were the Mandingoes and, Krans- tribes, many who took side with government. On the other hand, government troops hunted for Gio and Mano tribes. The situation was fragile because people spoke dialects of the other tribes. Inter-tribal marriages in Liberia were on the rise. It was impossible for any faction to demonstrate effectively who the real enemies were except for those they knew and could easily identify. Families were completely eliminated with no survival left to tell the story because of resentment one group over the opposing group. With the craziness that was going on, I watched and remembered the things I saw because I thought I would have the opportunity to sit and register what I experienced during the Liberian Civil War. And that is what I did.

Reading has been one of my habits since I was a child; I wanted to be around educated people most of the times that had access to books I could read and could digest what I read to improve some of what I acquired from reading into life and by reading I was able to learn some things about life; about those who made history, and how they passed their knowledge from one generation to another.

Some of the world's greatest men came from poor families, yet they overcame their circumstances. I realize I could do the same with God's help. I saw that among the least came some of best. Newspapers, libraries, magazines, or anything I was provided I read and visit. This was my life and it is still a very big portion of my habit. Education is like a stream of river that never runs dry. So, I will keep on learning as long as God is giving me the time to do so.

As a child, I dreamed of becoming a zoologist because of my love for nature and animals. In college, I wanted to do Political Science as a major but that too came to change. The civil war drove me to discover who I was born to be.

Refugee in Guinea

After I graduated from high school in Guinea, I started to notice more about my interests and skills. I also got some clues of what my choice of career would be.

I had experience as a humanitarian assisting with charities after our traumatic experience during the Liberia and Sierra Leone civil war. The potential for philanthropy in the future is something I pray for God to help me do if I am in the position to offer direct aid. It is critical to provide services to the cause of mankind in any little way possible, and in a unique and compassionate manner. I humbly request that God grants me this wish and blesses me with the funds to fulfill this dream. I like reading and writing a lot. I also had the hope someday that I could write and share our story with the world so that it could gain an awareness of the tragedy of the Liberian conflict. There are at least two sides to any story, and how we interpret those narratives is what matters the most. As a writer, it is not an easy task to undertake, but I did find out that I like writing more than talking. During my junior and senior years of high school, I always expressed my feelings to young ladies through writing. In most cases, their responses were positive. Also, I meditate a lot. Trying to see things through the eyes of the people around us could help us to understand what they are going through. Writing can be a gift for some who also work hard to bring such blessing to light. The only thing about having such a gift is that it could bring both sadness and happiness. It turns out bittersweet like this sometimes because nowadays writing is often underestimated for its subtleties. On top of this, there are the things we see happening in our world. One can't change the world with a single word. We can accomplish progress through collective effort. That is what I wish we could champion most in life is the possibility for improvement through cooperation.

The more that I continued to read over the years, the more my plan of becoming a writer was about to take shape. One question I kept asking myself was how good of a writer could I make myself. I was taught as a child growing up to be honest with myself and with others, but in life we all can make mistakes one way or the other. In all of my dealings with people, I try to learn and try my best to be forthright. In my writing, I want to sound clear and attempt to convey to my audience a message that I hope would help them find some balance and purpose in life. I am still asking God to bless me to contribute in making our world a peaceful place. I hope to do so through writing and by joining other peace loving people around the world.

It is often said that "there is power in positive thinking." It was time for a man, who like many other individuals who struggled through hardships, to recount those experiences in a tangible way in order to bring to life the horrors of the civil war, in other words to share his one story as a representative of the millions of other personal accounts of the violence and loss in Liberia. I hope my readers find what I have written useful and applicable in guiding others about the heartache, damage, and resilience of protracted civil war in West Africa.

I am now taking the first step. As someone once told me, "The height that great men reached was never done by a sudden flight but by sleepless days and nights." I kept this quotation close to my heart, and I hope to follow the same path that its wisdom advises. Here in this autobiography, I am doing my best as many predecessors did as narrative therapy following a war. I am following the footsteps of the men who have contributed some of their knowledge and time to enlighten the world. What is important is that the messages we have learned from scholars, philosophers and others, leaves us better prepared to make ethical and rational choices that could help make the world a better place. This, too, depends on the things we consider better, or how we define what is good in helping us to live in peace and justice.

Civil wars have left some countries in untenable positions in which they stand no chance to account for the entire physical toll, much less for the loss of life in these times of crisis. If we can prevent the escalation of violence, then we should do so without hesitation. It is important that we treat each other with respect and dignity.

While it is true people can ask for changes in a peaceful manner from their leaders, the citizens should also respect and abide by the laws of their nations. A major reason for this argument is that lawlessness can invite chaos. Millions of people around the world have shared tears and some could continue to do so because of some unexpected events in our world. God can bring peace to the entire world.

The Liberian Civil War

On August 1990 we arrived in Lofa on a bright sunny day with only few people left in the district of Foya. In Foya, I was eager to reach my uncle's house with the intension of meeting the other family members. Yes, I did see my uncle's daughter who was the first person I set eyes on after three years, since we last saw each other in the boarding school in Sierra Leone. Our encounter was very painful. She ran to me with open arms like a mother who was willing to embrace a lost child who has been away for years. I was so thin that one could see my bones under the skin. We hugged each other. I felt her tears running down my shoulders; it touched my heart so much. There is a saying in Sierra Leone that goes like this "a man is not supposed to cry." I knew no other way to hold back my tears.

For the first time, since my departure from Monrovia, I had a perfect shower, a well-prepared meal, and a comfortable bed to rest in after almost a month of walking days and nights. I ate as if I had never eaten anything before in my entire life. I was filled but refused to recognize my stomach was full.

My niece said she was worried and had no information whether I was dead or alive. No one confirmed the news about my state of being. You can see someone for about thirty minutes, but he or she could be dead within the next minute.

If I felt a sense of loneliness during the civil war it happened in Foya. Those I left in Foya were either killed by rebels or government troops. The entire district was almost completely deserted as the majority of its inhabitants migrated to the Guinean and Sierra Leonean borders. The towns and villages were deserted while others remained on the run to save their lives. What was left, were singing birds. I accepted the fact that the nation was at war with itself. This was a busy and noisy town but all the people had disappeared. I was back in the very town I had refused to return to early when my uncle asked me to do so. I was used to being a student in the city. I was young and didn't want to leave my friends behind. No regrets for coming back home, I knew what it was like to be home again. But to my disappointment as I went from house to house asking for those I knew, the responses were either; some had died or fled the area for their lives.

Many of the town dwellers now were forces loyal to Charles Taylor, head of the National Patriotic Front of Liberia. I dealt with the same faction on my leaving the city Monrovia. Here, I was again in the company of the same group after running away from the city center, Monrovia. The scenario was one could not completely live within any part of the country without dealing with the rebels. They were everywhere. I had to put my fear behind me to face the reality of the times. We were fed up with rebels and how they treated us. We needed some peace while in Foya, but the time to have real peace was far and we still had to withstand the challenges of the day.

My mind was made up to stay in Foya and not to go anywhere else. I was now willing to embrace the life of being home again. It was difficult dealing with the rebels in Lofa, especially child soldier. I was in the city where I saw heavy fighting and I didn't want things to be like that in Foya. In Foya, there was no resistance by remnants of the Arm Forces of Liberia when rebels entered and attacked the town. Government soldiers stationed in that part of the country had escaped to run for their lives. Rebels quickly took over the town. In the shortest possible time, they gathered women and girls. Many a fighter took two to three women for himself. For some, this was the first real time in their lives to take what they wanted. This triggered their eagerness and increased their appetites to take more of everything they could lay their eyes on.

The few men they met in Lofa were powerless and could do nothing to prevent rebels from taking even some of the precious values of the town. They simply took most of the women they encountered. Those who were armed were the tormentors. That was the order of the day. Either you accept their order or you pay for any rebellion against their rule. No one underestimated the power of the rebels. Some claimed they started the war from the Liberian, and Ivorian borders; so they thought they were the real commandos, well trained to fight any kind of warfare, because of the news received about them, they were held in high esteem.

For many, nothing was left to fear anymore. What some saw and witnessed in the city and along the way to Lofa was terrible. Many of us had the notion at the time, that life had no meaning during the civil war. From my understanding, we were headed in the wrong direction and peace was all we needed. Some civilian captured in their towns and villages were forced to join rebel factions to fight against the government forces, or other warring factions. Many were ill-fed and ill-clothed. Friends, who traveled with me to Lofy, had to trust the Lord to protect us along the way from any harm.

In Lofa, life was new again not as a normal society but the opposite. There was complete breakdown in law and order but a little better than what I saw in the city center. In Foya for some months one could live with rebels and have a relative peace of mind. We had to be attentive because fighting was still going on in some areas. There were always rumors of war. During those hard times, our lives wholly depended on the mercy of God which served as a source of empowerment and zeal to help us cope with the useless life we were now living. The rebels conducted a house to house search in the town of Foy and, according to them; they were searching for arms and ammunition left by forces of the AFL loyal to the late President Doe of Liberia. While it was true they had to search the entire district to make sure that the towns were free of other "enemy forces," some toke anything they thought had some value.

My life in Lofa improved and I gained weight because we could afford some food to eat. Food prices had tripled at this time. It was not a surprise to me; there were other people around the world who were in the same situation as us. My hope was that the war could come to an end so that we can go back to Monrovia and start life all over again. I dreamed of going back to school. This was the ambition of most young people trapped in the civil war. But the fighting would go on for more than fourteen years and a peace deal before anyone could think of living a normal life. Such life meant some of the worst predicaments of the time. The youth was the target of the day; the youth was recruited into the military and did almost all the fighting and killing as well, because the youth were forced and taught to do so. Life was entirely miserable in that barbaric and demonic era.

My heart never rested as I kept thinking of my family, friends, and neighbors in around Monrovia, including other parts of the country. Nights were troubling and long because of bad dreams. I kept having nightmares on a regular basis. My spirit was tormented by what was going on around me. I sat by the roadside, contemplating on the future in an anarchic society. A constant dream of peace was mere illusion and was not near at this time. For some of us, it was like coming from boiling water and going into a frying pan. Our lives, hopes, and dreams all rested on God. God, I knew, had the solution to the problems the country was facing.

With no elderly family member around to supervise us in Foya, we roamed around in search of some hope. One of my nieces took charge of the family's properties. She did so in the absence of my uncle and his wife. We had been caught in some of the world's dangerous and most brutal environments- Liberia. The rebels showed few signs of kindness or mercy.

My ears could no longer bear or hear the screaming and the pain of those who were being cruelly tortured. Some were begging rebels to show them mercy and to spare their lives. Weren't we brothers yesterday? But this time we were killing our own brothers and referring to them as enemies. Nothing much some could do, but we had to wait for a time when we could live together in peace again. We were living out of the context of a civilized society for that time period. We felt abandoned and left in the hands of the warlords for their use in the middle of the war. Some fled to the US, Europe or other places where there was peace. Some politicians left in Liberia joined hands with warlords to save themselves. They seemed to have forgotten they have misled us.

President Samuel Doe was prepared to go to war and destroy Liberia because he had lost respect by his own people. It was hard to accept and cope with the frustrating and psychological effect that we had to witness. The people whose families the rebels and government troops hurt, had to forgive and accept peace as the only solution.

At this time, of conflict, revenge killing and betrayal because of the war, it was better to return to the peace table and renew our vow to our beloved country. It was necessary that we forgive one another and foster solid reconciliation. Truer repentance had to come from the heart, and not only from talking. We had to be willing to battle corruption in high and low places because that was one of the fundamental reasons for the war in Liberia. We knew what it would take to bring hope and a brighter future to Liberia.

Setting my feet on the soil of Foya and running from the city center where the fighting was heavily concentrated, I felt it was a dream comes true. Here, I thought there would be no more fighting. I was wrong. Some of the worst fighting was yet to come, even in the interior. Those who were in Foya when the United Liberation Movement of Liberia for Democracy forces entered Foya, the lucky ones, fled in every direction. These fighters, like the others, demonstrated their intention to destroy and take full control of the country. Despite the fact that the people here did not take part in the fighting, their properties were still looted and destroyed, and their young women raped. Mandingo tribe people everywhere in Liberia were killed for some strange tribal reason.

The situation in Liberia was almost the same as what took place in Rwanda. The fighters in Liberia and Sierra Leone carried out the killings. They carried out the killings of their fellow citizens, or those from other tribes. In Rwanda, soldiers and civilians were deeply involved in the genocide. It did not make any sense.

Having spent two and half years in Foya, I tried to go back to school. I attended a refugee school established by some refugee teachers from Sierra Leone and Liberian. The goal of these teachers was to redirect young men and women into normal life, especially those who had taken up arms as a way of life. This goal was interrupted by rebels many times. The rebels demanded teachers to stop their teaching. They wanted to take us away to join their senseless deadly war game. It was very hard for the youth to achieve anything. There were constant harassments detentions and interruptions. This was during the occupation of Foya by NPLF forces.

ULIMO dissidents became another problem for us in Foya. For those who were left behind to tell what transpired, it was not a good storyline. Some people around the world have experienced this sad unrest. The fighting in Lofa lasted months with many killed and many fled into exile in the surrounding countries, of Africa or abroad.

I am grateful to God and those who made it possible for some of us to cross into Guinea after several attempts to cross the river dividing Liberia and Guinea while hoping to seek refuge had proved unsuccessful. My older sister was already in Guinea where she had sought refuge and tried many times to see me with the intention for me to cross into Guinea.

I have been blessed to listen to my instincts and not overlook what came to mind. In Foya, I knew something was about to happen. It was in the form of a revelation. I cannot recall the entire dream but one thing I did not forget for sure was that the town was attacked and destroyed. People were crying and running for their lives. When ULIMO attacked Foya, according to some who left behind, it was brutal. They spared women they had interest in and those who escaped. It was difficult for a rational person to explain what was happening at that time.

Some had to design a strategy to escape Foya to go to the Guinean border for safety. While it was true ULIMO forces were far from capturing the town, some of us had to prepare before they got close to town. I took this issue seriously and made haste to leave the town. It was like Sodom and Gomorrah; some had the choice to stay in Lofa with the fighters loyal to Charles Taylor, which too was a risk.

Upon hearing ULIMO's plans not to spare any living thing in Foya, that was enough to convince many to flee the town as soon as we could. As for those rebels, I got used to them while we were living together in Foya before the district fell to ULIMO, although I had problem trusting them for a few reasons. They wanted to force us to fight for them against the government troops. Many chose not to fight or to kill innocent people or peasants. We couldn't rely on them to protect us.

There was a point of contention on many occasions between the rebels and some young people who refused to take part in the fighting. I had to be careful and to be on the alert. In such times, some became a one-man army fighting to survive any kind of attack coming from our brothers. I was asked the same hypothetical question repeatedly by some of the rebels in Foya; like "Where would you go or hide in case our enemies were to attack our position? "You have nowhere to go," some would say. On that day you will be forced to fight on our side or we will execute you." My response was always, "I have nowhere to run or to hide. The only thing I will have to do is to fight alongside you guys." Most of them laughed and responded by saying,

"You have no choice but to fight or you are dead." Some of us had to say it in that manner because we wanted to survive the civil war.

I felt I had no one on my side but God. He was my last and only hope. Every evening I bowed down and prayed as I was taught to do since my childhood by my parents. I decided to sketch a map of the route I could use to leave once and for all. It was not a map that I could carry with me. So I needed a cognitive map like many in Foya, using the simplest and easiest routes most people could rarely think of using. Many people started making plans ahead of time, thinking what to do. The right thing for those who were living in Foya at the time was leaving early and not to forcedly join the rebels to fight and to kill innocent people. I asked God for guidance.

I spent time to study my survey plan of the exact route and time for my trip. My plan to leave the town was ready to be implemented. I knew for sure we had to be attentive to anything around us. Escaping the town was the only way out for many. There was no retreat or surrender. Some had to leave even if it meant using the thickest jungles and bushes. We had to travel at night where no one would suspect the plan. The first thing I thought of was to take nothing heavy with me, on this long journey. This plan was simple. I kept my posture as I always did. That is being peaceful. This was a tactical move.

We had to stay calm and friendly toward the fighters. I knew for sure we could not trust the rebels around us completely. We the civilians wanted to leave the town to avoid the fighting. We had to be careful to watch out for them. Even our movement and path in the dark was well planned. We wanted no surprise on our way to the boarder. Like many in Foya, I was a fugitive now because I did not take part in the national rebellion and to do so, meant, we would have to participate in the killing of innocent Liberians.

I had God on my side. I could feel his ever presence around me. In the wake of all of the ordeals that continued to take a toll on my life since my childhood and continued to affect me during every stage of the civil war God served as a source of my strength, courage, determination, persistence, and endurance. Some of us were making every effort to have a stable life but the war was still going on. What were the reasons for all the troubles and problems? I needed answers from somebody. I could not predict but kept on in the search for these answers.

Upon arrival in Foya, many believed it was saved and would have some peace of mind. We were wrong. The civil war was only taking the worst turn. By this time, the only areas left for trading and some sense of life were Guinea and Sierra Leone. These two countries border Foya, where we got our basic survival needs. Back in the days when I was a student in Sierra Leone I knew how kind the people were to us. I will always be grateful to them for the years I spent there.

The Liberian and Sierra Leone Civil War would have some impact on the region. The ramifications were devastating and caused many to die. Did Sierra Leone do anything wrong to its Liberian neighbor? It was victimized as well. It was all a dreadful mistake. The price was costly. The war created further poverty. This was real. It was no fun. Many saw destruction of property and human lives. No one told us the stories about what was taking place on the ground. Who could put an end to what was happening to the people of these two nations? When I was alone, it was like a movie replaying in my dreams both day and night of the horrible ways in which children, parents and families were killed by their own people. These were families from one end of the border to the other. Those were the same people with whom they lived together with in towns and villages, who were now their attackers and killers.

Some fighters from both Liberia and the Sierra Leone's Civil Wars were children who had no experience in doing almost anything a sound minded person would do. Who can we blame? Innocent children once lived with their parents. Some went to school and others went to the farm with their parents. They were brought up in decent, peaceful, and loving homes. They knew nothing about guns or warfare. The children wanted to live a normal live with their parents. They wanted a better future and to be able to help some of their poor families. Some parents did every, and almost anything to make sure their children were in school. But their plans were unfulfilled. Their plans were replaced by nightmare and brutality.

These were killers we were living among; they were now in control because they had guns. Their victims had no power. Those of us who did not carry arms or did not participate in arms conflict in Liberia and Sierra Leone only sat and watched how they treated helpless and innocent people. Liberians had relatives in Guinea and Sierra Leone. We were border families. The destruction, killing, and looting, brought hopelessness to the people of these two sister nations. However, we should not forget that those who took part in the fighting many, if not the majority, were decent people before the war. That is way we should forgive each other and put past behind us to embrace peace.

Because of the fighting, at some point, I forgot my identity. That part of me which made me human, disappeared for some time, and there, I stood, trying to understand what just took place. I thought how many people were killed. "Am I going to be the next victims?" I asked myself. I felt less of a human being.

I was not different. I was alive because of God's mercy. Tears, I had no more to share. People were being killed one after the other, or in a large number.

I joined the border cross trade in Foya to get food to survive. The inhabitants of Foya and those who came from other parts of Liberia to seek refuge in that area could only survive by trading in Guinea and Sierra Leone, which was before rebels invaded that Sierra Leone. When rebels invaded Sierra Leone the only place left was Guinea. It was a struggle to save one's own life. We were surrendered by gunmen on every side who took orders from their commanders. Some of the fighters could not read or write. These fighters we had to be mindful of.

A child solider, with little or no thinking capability of his own, worsened the situation and endangered many more lives. Sad, we were there at the time to witness such evil development. In this terrible state I forgot to know what life was worth. What happened was no fiction. It was no high school graduation, but a once peaceful nation at war with itself. Like many, I was surrounded by madness. It could have been prevented. Was this a biblical revelation? Was the Bible fulfilling itself? It was like doom's day for people caught in a killing spree. Was this the end of time? I completely lost my mind. I waited for answers that had no specific time.

A bloody war that lasted fourteen years took from us that which our parents had worked for, for decades. Our support line was taken away from us like a thief at night. Our rights were taken away and we were abused by the rebels. As civilians, there was nothing we could do. Reconciliation may be a meaningful way for us. Only God can decree judgment accordingly. Our loved ones killed during the civil wars, we have to keep their memories. Our sufferings were countless and senseless. My childhood was rapidly transformed from that of a lad to a wandering person during the fighting. Parents provided for their children in the best way and brought them stability, but that time came to an end when the civil war started. We had to look forward to better days. Now, all we wished for was stability after the civil war. Poverty was now at our front door.

The Liberian Civil War made the situation even harder and more frustrating for us. The civil war drove many out of Monrovia and some made it to various Counties in Liberia. I made it to Foya. This was the birth place of my dad. The area is close to Sierra Leone and Guinean's borders. It was the best place to be while war descended on Liberia.

Was the Guinea government ready to receive refugees from Liberian and Sierra Leone, with thousands of Liberians who were fleeing weekly? Guinea was the only place that made sense. Liberia was the mother of war by now. The Guinean authority was strong and could not turn a blind eye on refugees entering its borders. The situation was abnormal and fragile. We were too many to add our problems to the people of Guinea, with their own problems they were undergoing. It was a difficult situation that could not be avoided. We were ready to risk anything to stay alive. Some made it across the border into Guinea. If you were accused, for having connections to the rebels only had to do with the commanders on the ground and the men under them.

At some point in time, some us needed some money to cross into Guinea. The risk to survive and the requirement were high. For some of us, we had no choice, but to make some sacrifices. Reflecting on my life for the past twenty years the death of my dad forced me to move from one place to another, living with family members or friends. It was the only thing to do; I also had to accept the struggles along the way to stay alive. I asked God many times why this was happening to me. That was just one chapter of my life. The Liberian Civil War opened a different chapter that became the worst chapter not only for me but for many Liberians as well. I had desired this burdensome period to be over and gone forever. I was tired and needed a break. I had to wait to see when this chapter would close. My childhood was shattered and long gone. Only years of sad memories were left. Stories of the Liberian Civil War were terrifying and left bad memories on those who witnessed it. I am thankful to God that many of us are still around.

This is my beloved grandma from my
mother side who passed away few years
after my departure from Liberia in 2003.
She understood what humility meant.

The author is seen in this photo researching for his book
during a visit at Barns & Noble in New York.

My mother, seen here in this photo,
is fasting and praying, along with
other women for peace to return to
Liberia after the bloody civil war
that claim so many lives

My late mother, as usual, is giving
thanks and praises to God, despite
the setbacks that have ravaged our
family and nation –a wonderful
mother who had given her all even
when it was her last.

The author is hanging out at the only supply
water line for the Kunnin's refugee camp
in Guinea.

The author is standing at
the pump with a refugee,
where the camp inhabi-
tants came to get water.
The author is standing at
the pump with a refugee,
where the camp inhabi-
tants came to get water.

Titus is seen very excited with a
co-worker after landing a job as a
social worker after graduation from
high school in 1989.

The author is taking a
stroll through Nongoa's
refugee camp in Guinea,
one of the camps where he
once worked.

The author is celebrating with friends and family members during a high school graduation ceremony.

Jubilating with high school classmates shortly after the West African Examination Council, (WAEC) exams in Guinea.

The author in this photo is contemplating about life, and what the future holds for thousands of other refugees like himself

The author is in this photo with co-workers during distribution of non-food items to the refugees.

Jubilating with high school classmates shortly after the West African Here, mother is seen in her choir gown. She served as a member of the native choir in the Church of Pentecost in Liberia.

The author is receiving his high school diploma in 1998.

The author is standing between three best friends, from the second person on the left and to the last on the right.

My father, Robert Saah Bendu Ngaieh, who was in this late 40's before his untimely death in 1983.

Border - Cross in Guinea

It was now four years since the inception of the civil war and I was living in the largest county. My father was born here, as I said and with continuous talk of another rise of rebel faction on its way to attack the town of Foya, one of the few districts left, was clear. Nowhere in Liberia was safe. The rest of the towns in Foya had almost entirely fallen to one of the warlords, ULIMO. This group was in Foya, where I was stationed at the time. It was time for me to leave Foya and go into exile in Guinea, once and for all. This was not something I had anticipated doing or had imagined I would do. I wanted to stay and to live in Foya with the rebels and the people I was used to. It was just too tough trusting the Guinean soldiers for fear I would be treated like one of the combatants.

Unconfirmed report from those who were involved in the cross border trade between Liberia and Guinea, made things even worse for some to risk attempt crossing into Guinea. Soldiers were arresting those whom they believed had links to NPFL rebels. There were mistakes about that based on false identity or misinformation.

There were also many scary stories to discourage many who wanted to seek refuge in Guinea. That was the case with me. However, thousands of refugees were allowed to cross into Guinea. It was impossible for anyone to stop that kind of exodus. For women, it was a different issue because of their sympathy towards their gender. For men, it was more of a risk. For those Liberians who used to trade with the Guinea before the civil war, had family members in Foya, they had to get them out to cross into that country regardless of the risk. The heart-breaking risk for some who made it across the Guinean border was for someone to point them out. I calculated the risk in Guinea as high. Even though some had no direct affiliation with either side in the conflict, I still needed to be careful not to be falsely accused. Why would I think the Guineans would set me free after crossing their border in consideration of my youth? Why should they trust me and the stories I would tell them, distinguish me from young rebels around my age at the time.

My decision to cross into Guinea was tough, but the risk was necessary and worth it. My chances of surviving another risk by another group of fighters were still high. We were compelled to leave Foya. My decision not to partake in the fighting, or to side with any of the groups served as a tangible evidence of good decision for life. The craziest thing was getting caught in crossfire, which many didn't want to risk. In this dilemma, it was appropriate to think and plan well.

My uncle's family was in Guinea, seeking refuge and praying for God's mercy to bring me back to them safely. I was the only one in the family in still in Liberia, where fighting was heavily concentrated. My mother, with three of my brothers, and two sisters were away for more than few years since she left me in Monrovia. I had to spend additional four years away from them.

If anyone needed a miracle to survive the war I was one of them. We were yearning for some kind of divine intervention. Like many, I was fleeing for my life in every corner or direction I considered was safe. Many people had to travel through bushes, forest, and had to climb hills, escaping the fighting because some didn't want to be blamed for taking the life of another, which was my major fear in the entire civil war. Anyone could take up arm to fight alongside any of the rebel groups and my point was clear. Who was fighting whom? We were the same people killing and looting each other's homes. This made no sense to me at all. I rather stay on the run to save my life form those hostile rebel groups, than to kill my own brothers and sisters. To stay alive, many spent days without food, safe drinking water, and security protection.

Being with the rebels, you had some false sense of security protection. I knew that kind of protection was not guaranteed. It was only temporary. We wanted to fine a safe place with no worries about gunmen running after us and forcing us to do what they wanted. It was never a choice of life for many. We wanted to make our own decisions and to have the opportunity to do things we wanted to. Putting our fear aside and trusting God, was the only thing some could do. It was clear: to either stay on the run and never to join the arm struggle or kill in the war to survive. Compromising my beliefs was the last thing on my mind. Many Liberians wanted to be free with no blood on their hands. Thinking about the guilt, if one took the life of others who had no part in the fighting. I tried to wonder how it would be. It was like a picture put on the wall of my mind I couldn't easily erase.

Confident my plan was set to leave Foya, I wanted no change of mind, or to come up with another plan of action. Who wanted to spend a life time running away from his past? We found ourselves in this predicament because the nation was headed in the wrong direction due to errors and this brought about the civil war. We were on the run constantly during the fighting hoping the table would turn in our favor, to reunite with our families. We had no time to sit and think about those who misled us to this road. Our thoughts at the time were mostly focused on how we could live to see another day. What we were going to eat for each passing day was our paramount concern. Where we could find safe drinking water, was equally important to our overall health. One could see the desperation on our faces, waiting and hoping for a radical change in the right direction for the nation, and the future of its people.

I walked for almost a month, escaping the fighting in the Liberian capital and after four years of fighting, there we were still on the run. 'When was all of this stuff going to be over," I asked. Guinea could be the place and country that would bring some kind of relief to some of us. There, I discovered a new beginning and a different kind of struggle. This was the beginning of chapter three in my life.

There were challenges awaiting refugees in Guinea we never dreamed of. Many refugees were moving with no giving up on life. In those daring times, I was aware life would change somewhere or someday. Those were moments of torment for many refugees. We were tortured by the different circumstances we were surrendered by. We couldn't tell what was going to happen later the next day or night and continuing to function as a normal person during the war, was beyond my own comprehension. Those who survived the civil war, we are still thankful to God for protecting us. How and why some made it alive, God alone knows the answer? He is my redeemer and my provider. The fighting in Liberia took more than fourteen years.

No one could ever believe it would have lasted that long. Those years for Liberians were wasted years. No one can replace what we lost, especially the youth.

Many Liberians and friends from Sierra Leone spent some years languishing in refugee camps, in and around Guinea, including countries in Africa. Those who were fortunate to escape the country at the start of the war had the upper hand to pursuit their goals and dreams in life. For those of us who were left behind only relied on our faith; God kept us safe and alive. I saw more than I am able to narrate. There were incidents I saw that knocked me off my feet. I came to my senses when all was over. The good times and good life for many Liberians came to an end because of the civil war. I reflected on the past of my father when he was alive. I remembered the good life with my family. There were times we wore the same outfit to church, and on other occasions we went together with our parents especially our dad.

He was educated and had many good friends. He had many friends who came around to visit. The beautiful women he met with well-paid jobs were some of his friends and close associates. The little birthday parties we had at home were gone and over. The shopping, the buying, the Christmas, and New Year celebrations with friends and neighbors were no more. The toys we got as gifts for holidays, the new clothes, the sharing of gifts, were memories I now carried with me in the War.

I was little when he passed away but I understood the importance of education and how it counted for some of the good life some people enjoyed. So I wanted education. We prayed for better days. We the children wanted to be happy, go to parties with friends, and have our family around again. We wanted to attend school without fear of guns' sound, or gunmen trying to hurt or kill others. It was too late. The things of the past became memories to last a lifetime. I wanted to look at life from another side. Those times with my parents and all that they provided us were over. My only hope in life was God and the good people he had along the way in this life to help.

My parents didn't forsake us nor did they fail to live up to their responsibility as parents. It just happened to be one of those times in life, when you can't define what was going on at the time. I was now like an outcast or the cow with no tail. My life was miserable and I felt I was nobody. My thoughts of years without my parents were no more than recollection of the past. Yet, I was alive, strong, and well intelligent to keep my head up high, trusting God for his grace.

Having spent a month hanging around on the Liberian side of the border, I had at least a picture of what I was going into. Not all refugees crossing into Guinea had to pay. Some were lucky. For me and many more, we paid $30.00 US and more.

The fact is one had to pay his custom fee for entering a country. We were on the run to save the life in us, and that was the most important thing. The UN and other international organizations were involved in making sure thousands of refugees made their way over the border into Guinea. Crossing the border into Guinea was the only option left. Many had nothing except life. The clothes I wore were not worthy for exchange. I can't recall wearing a decent foot wear on my feet during this time. They were of no use any way. Food was our desired focus. Everyone wanted to eat to survive another day. Material stuff was of no consequence. Life was more important than material possession.

Many people left behind their possession for their life. Focusing on the danger at the time was the only thing for us.

All I truly desired was to reunite with my family and friends. The few well-to-do kids I hanged out with once in a while made no sense any more. I was learning what life is worth. The trauma we went through still haunts us. Many Liberian including me, waited for a month on the border, for some kind of miracle one could provide a rescue operation to take us to Guinea. There, I would experience a peace once again. Liberia was entirely infected with various methods for killing for the next fourteen years. I had hoped to get out at once and for good. I was like a watchman watching his master in the middle of the night. It seemed like the story of "Daniel in the Bible," waiting to be delivered from the lion's den.

Every day that passed by left us more frustrated and tried to find a resting-place for the life in us. Many waited for many days and nights, wishing for a family member or a friend. Also, I waited impatiently for God. I prayed every day and night. I was not the only person waiting for this breakthrough. There were hundreds and hundreds who waited to cross into Guinea in order to start a new life. God was our only hope.

My older sister who was now in Guinea visited the border to ensure she found her boyfriend. It was during that same time she was asked by my uncle to find me.

According to my sister, she had been around the border for weeks to find her boyfriend and me, but as the saying goes, "blood is thicker than water, whether she would find me first or her boyfriend.

The South African reggae legend, Lucky Dube, in one of his songs, said, "Love is thicker than blood, which" is true, but the power of love was also played as usually in this situation. This was a very tough decision to make. The reason she found herself in that dilemma was because she could not afford the money for our traveling expenses. She was given a specific amount by uncle to facilitate my easy passage into Guinea. Whether my sister would betray her boyfriend for me that was the question? He meant everything to her. As the saying goes, "Family stick can bend, but can't break." This was my blood sister and there was no way I was willing to give up on her as well.

It was left with me to figure out why my sister acted the way she did. All went well and she was successful in finding her boyfriend before me. I waited around the Liberian broader, wishing for a while to hear my name. My sister was desperate and so was I. No day was promised to live on the border. We could hear heavy guns sound and the fighting gradually approached us. My sister had to find a way to get money to find me quickly. Time was of the essence. She was deeply worried. I was her blood brother and she could not afford to lose me, or she would answer to the rest of the family, regarding the money she received to find me.

I was hanging around the boarder one afternoon when I heard my name echoed from the Guinea border. My sister had to identify me because many people wanted to cross. It was a victory, but a temporary one. We had friends and relatives behind rebel line and they too needed some help and we had to find their location.

As I sat on the boat crossing into Guinea, it was like a new beginning in my troubled life. It was incredible that I was out of Liberia after almost five years of civil unrest. I had a lot on mind. My concern was not all about me. I was thinking about the friends and people I was leaving behind. It was my hope they live to see another day while I was gone? I prayed and cried in my heart. I was happy and sad at the same time. Some had no family member in Guinea to help them cross to safety. I was leaving behind lives that were dear to me. If there were anything I could do I will not hesitate to come in. What was their future in a lawless country where no one could be held accountable? Some Liberians later gained entrance in Guinea. Those with fire power in Liberia were masters of the day. What they said were final. It was a hopeless and uncertain environment.

`This burden was heavy on my shoulders. Liberians and Sierra Leoneans, who waited to gain entrance into Guinea, had to decide what they wanted to do with their lives. Here, at the border, they waited to cross into Guinea. How sad it was looking into eyes as they sat across the border. They lost everything and the only thing they had left was life.

The Guineans were not responsible for Liberian and Sierra Leone problems. They were at their borders to protect the interest of their country and people. The Guinean authority had to protect their borders because it could not easily distinguish between rebels and civilians. We all dressed in civilians outfit. Liberians who were fortunate and blessed to gain entrance into Guinea, had their own stories to share, and those who never got the upper hand to cross before the arrival of the rebels, had their own version, too. Those who left behind, not by choice were because time was not in their favor. When rebels came to the border, some were forced to join the fighting or carry loads for the rebels. These loads included arms and ammunition as well as food, if there was any. It was a setback and hopeless situation for those innocent Liberians and Sierra Leonean.

I was finally in Guinea as refugee for my life. Here, I learned the real meaning of being a refugee. The environment was different and the people spoke many languages, including French as the national language. To fit in that society one had to be assimilated first. This process was not an easy task for us. I wanted go back to school and complete high school. So, many challenges awaited us in this new environment. I needed time to recuperate from pain of the war. This was the kind of environment I have longed for.

Liberians hoped that peace and stability could return soon but it almost seemed impossible to think life would return to normal.

I wanted to go back to school and to finish high school. I needed to work hard to catch up. Some friends I knew in Liberia had further advanced in school. I wasn't going to give up. I had to be strong to peruse my goal and go back to school to help my family someday.

The refugee status was not an easy life to cope with. Little food, no fixed income, or no job to sustain oneself became an issue. This was another battle we had to fight just to survive. This time, it wasn't a struggle to escape from gunmen or the rebels. It was another predicament to fit into a society that was preoccupied with tons of its own problems. Guineans were barely trying to survive. Can one imagine how difficult it must have been for refugees in a different culture? We were caught up in this whole fiasco.

Guinea is rich in natural resource, but many people lived in poverty. If Liberia was normal I rather choose to be home than to live as refugee in Guinea. Here we were caught up in Guinea, waiting for the mess that would last for years in Liberia to come to an end. Countless numbers of those killed or feared missing were facts of the war stories. Our stories and experiences of war will pass on one generation to another.

The United Nation and the Red Cross, in collaborating with the Guinean authority, came to the aid of some Liberian and Sierra Leone refugees. I was one of them. Few refugee schools were built in towns where refugees stationed.

In Gueckedou, I went back to school for the first time after spending nearly five years in Liberia. In Guinea, I looked for ways to pursue my dreams. The school environment was very strange because my mind was clouded by harsh reality on the ground in Liberia. I was determined to face challenges and to accept the constraints that came with it. We walked two to three miles to get to school. At times, we had no food and no money on hand. We only managed to get by on a daily basis. Many dropped out form school in Guinea. I stayed in there with the others. I made it and came out from High school successfully. There were times I went to bed with no food at all.

If I had to push myself to go to school, it was worth making the sacrifice to achieve that goal. One thing I knew for sure was that my dad was dead and gone and my mother was nowhere around. I had to make use of the little assistance my uncle and his wife could provide. Food was very important but not enough to fully keep us sane. It was clear to me and I understood what was going on. We had to embrace those times and to appreciate what we had. Our life style changed dramatically. In Guinean we were a little better off than some refugee's families. Things and times were to change for a while.

As a high school graduate, I needed something to do. I could not afford to just sit around with no opportunity. I was happy that I made it through high school, as the first person from my family. My dad was long dead and gone. My dad left my mother with five young boys in addition to two girls and a boy she had with another man she married after Dad's death. I had no clue what my sisters looked like. I have been away for years.

Opportunity soon came my way–a job with a nongovernmental organization, operated under the auspices of the United Nations to attend to needs of Liberians and Sierra Leone's refugees in Guinea. I was chosen for the position of a Social worker. I was very fortunate, "To God be the glory". It was like being the only man with one eye to help many helpless people. I was going to earn a pay on a check monthly basis for the first time in my life after graduating. I was fascinated and encouraged to do my best to get the job done and on time.

Some friends and family members quickly turned to me for help. Their problems were enormous and my income could not do much. This, too, brought lots of stress on me. I wanted to help as many people as I could, but with little resources, I could not accomplish much. However, it was a chance to do something provided and an unforgettable experience for me. As a high school graduate, I had one foot in the world and the other on the journey to experience. I needed to grow and to get a clear picture of the world I was now a part of. The challenge to fit into a society with limited experience was a herculean challenge. I was just about to learn something new and get to know how cold this world could be. It was a new learning process. Some say, "it's common sense', but how common? I was about to know. I had to learn the hard way, even though I wanted to do it the easy way. There is no easy way in life.

My first assignment was to go to one of the surrounding villages around the Gueckedou region, a district in Guinea where some Liberian and Sierra Leonean refugees were based. I had no objection but to accept the assignment. One major reason for taking this assignment was that many Guineans and thousands of refugees were hungry and in need. I was excited to some extent, but not quite sure I wanted to go that far. I was leaving the town with all my friends and loved ones to take on this new assignment, where I would spend months. It was my choice and it was worth the attempt. So I went and left the rest behind.

Working with refugees had required a high level of scrutiny. The kind of suffering I witnessed in those refugee camps was heart-breaking. It was beyond human imagination. Today I can't fathom the reason, and how to describe this degradation. I guess it was the first time in my life, seeing this senseless and mass displacement of people in my entire life. People were living with almost no hope of recovering from their losses. I did not know how to make sense of the matter.

It was a hopeless situation. How we got there? It felt like war had started within me, itching just to find some answers. On many nights, it was difficult to get a good rest after a hard day work. We worked from 6: am morning to 8 pm distributing UN food for refu-gees. There really was no sleep most of the nights, remembering the faces of malnourished women and children. Watching the sick with wounds that seemed to have no cure was even worse. Shortage of food, medical supplies for people of refugee status, seemed too much to keep up on the job as much as I wanted to.

You could predict how long a person or sick refugee would take his or her last breath by the looks and agony written on their face. Sometimes, we worked very late to respond to these desperate sit-uations with the hoped no one was left out. No matter how long we worked in extra hours, it could not help meet the thousands of ref-ugees who needed help. I am talking about three to four hundred thousand refugees in one location, with many more close to sur-rounding villages.

There was too much to see, too much to do, too much to bear, and too many people to serve at the same time. But this very difficult responsibility seemed too overwhelming, burdensome to effectively handle. No one could ease the refugee's pain in the manner they hoped, only but God.

For me, it was a great honor to serve helpless refugees. As one of the world's brilliant men Albert Einstein, said, "Only a life lived for others is a life worthwhile." So I have no regret. It was the best choice, place and time for me to serve. I have learned to appreciate life even more because some never had a second chance at life. How do you forget something of this nature when you were there? Insufficient food, the lack of nutrition and inadequate standard of living, lack of such provisions did not help them to fight the kind of sicknesses and diseases that were easily curable. Attempt to help was the significant experience of the entire mission. Refuges waited for donor countries and individuals for assistance to reduce their suffering. Seniors and infants were the most vulnerable.

Working for refugees was a crucial task. I will never forget how I felt, being in that environment. Refugees were driven from their homes unwillingly. Some family members were killed by rebels; others were abducted and forced into battle.

Liberian and Sierra Leonean refugees were forced into exile. Some will never get to know the truth about the deaths of their love ones. Such had been the case with my senior brother, whose disappearance brought us no answer as to how he was killed or where he might be after more than fourteen years. I had to deal with many challenges at work, but it was still very rewarding for someone fresh from high school. It became another form of learning experience. It was the first step, in becoming a social worker, knowing how to treat one's clients with respect, care and not being judgmental. This made more sense. If you want to be treated this way, you must learn how to do the same for others. I was highly inspired to work when I started the job, but I had to deal with those I met on the job and follow their wisdom. Understanding the way refuges responded to services they received was unusual as a beginner. They were very upset at times with the quality; of food. They seemed to forget it was not about quality, it was only meant for them to survive.

This was a tough situation for anyone to deal with, but one could understand their frustrations. It was not their fault, living under such conditions. Here, they waited for someone to decide when to feed them and the kind of food they would receive. It was sad being there, watching them. But don't forget I was one of them, too. So, I had to be patient to deal with their anger. Furthermore, this was my job so I had to put up with it.

After spending few months on the job, I was transferred to another refugee camp, an hour and a half drive away from Gueckedou, a Guinea district, where most of the locals and international NGOs in that region established their headquarters.

I began my assignment in a nearby Guinea village called Nonkowa. This was another strange place for me. My new assignment, I was given some hints about the town, the people who lived there, and to be mindful when dealing with them. Some Guineans just didn't want to be bothered with refugees. There were some nice people there, however some Guineans didn't want to see refugees living and working among them, where most of them had no jobs. We had no voice or power. We were vulnerable and helpless. We had few rights in a country that had gone out of its way to give us sanctuary.

Their economy was very dry. Our presence as refugees perhaps worsened their own situation. True too, that there were lots of positive things going on in Guinea because of the presence of Liberian and Sierra Leonean refugees there. New roads were constructed or old ones were remodeled. Some shelter homes for refugees provided or created some sort of livelihood for Guinean citizens.

Guineans were given first preference on employment basis. It made sense because we were in their country and this eased some of the tensions that were built up between our host country and the refugees. I realized that confusion, at times, left little or no room for any rational thinking. However, the answer was simple, the Guineas, nor we the refugees, were going anywhere. Refugees and Guineans lived together for a time, and accepted each other if we wanted to survive as a people.

We had to put away our differences and find that which made us common as human beings. In those critical times, we needed to hold to our peace as we did home. Despite the problems that existed between refugees and Guineans, life went on. The refugees, who were not fortunate, paid the price with their lives or torture or imprisonment. The Guinean government plate was filled with cases between refugees and their citizens. There were many problems on ground. Amidst all these obstacles, many still had hope. No difficulty was going to deter some from keeping up with life, except for God.

The advice I received from those who knew the town prepared me to survive there. This was another country with their beliefs and way of life. So I needed to take heed and not get caught up in any problem I would come to regret. Trouble is something we sometimes try to run away from, but could fine us at times.

I tried my best not to look for trouble in Guinea but there were times it seemed I was blinded to certain things or problems coming my way.

In my new role as the youngest social worker, another form of problem developed in my work area. This was not something I expected nor was I ready for it as a new employee with less experience on the Job. My goal at the time was to learn everything on the job and to equip myself. As refugees, we were constantly watched by authorities and their citizens, most especially those with some job skills. We were looked down upon by some Guineans, and we were called many names, but I think this was done out of ignorance or illiteracy. For those who knew better, fully understood what we were going through as a people. My first month on the job was ok but it was equally sad to see thousands of refugees stranded.

The Liberian Civil War and the rebel movement in Sierra Leone, added more responsibilities to the UN and other humanitarian organizations around the world. Problems in refugee camps regarding fairness of UN rations sometimes ended in commotion. Refugee's population was huge and the means to feed everyone was equally difficult. Many refugees' foods were stolen. Those involved some, were never caught or punished. The question was: what were we doing in Guinea? Which factor led us here? Was it the result of a perished Liberia?

Before my second assignment came up I bought a puppy dog for company. As a child, my dad always kept dogs in our home. Even before his untimely death, we had two dogs. Dogs during my childhood had always been my pet best friend. Here, I was now with one of my own. I wanted a dog after the death of my father, but I could not afford to keep one because of my age. In addition to that came, the civil war, which made it difficult to maintain a steady civil society. Dogs are very special. When I walked the streets in towns, cities, counties, I always admired dogs when I saw them with their owners.

Accepting my next assignment in the Guinean town of Nonkowa meant I had to take my job more seriously. I had to count on advice given me by refugees who worked in these towns before me, regarding some knowledge of refugees and their host countries. I was warned to take it easy to avoid any problem. The refugee camp was not far away from where I lived. So I spent most of my free time there to avoid cross path with the Guinea soldiers heavily deployed around villages. The soldiers were sent there to make sure rebels from Liberia and Sierra Leone did not trespass into the Guinean side.

Even though I liked to dress neatly for work I was discouraged to do that because many refugees could not afford to buy new clothes. Living among refugees, I realized the job was not one you expect happiness over pity. This kind of life was sad and very hard to cope with, seeing human suffering around. These refugees were people; it was wise not to overly distinguish oneself. I distributed some of my clothes, which I did with no hesitation. Guineans are very good at making sure they identify strangers among them no matter how you dress. They had to be cautious because their neighbors were going through a civil crisis. Some Guinean citizens blamed Liberians for their problems and they were right. We could do nothing but to wait for peace to return to Liberia. The Guineans were suspicious of the young men residing among them. Allegations of rebels were made against this group on some occasions. Many refugees were arrested and sent to prison. Others were tortured and some never came back. So, we were losing our young ones. Refugees who were already wearied from the Civil War in Liberia and Sierra Leone tried to avoid any more of this danger. Too much was going on. We were living by the mercy of God. It felt at times that our lives were just on the balloon. Some of us are still grateful for surviving the times we lived there, and the good and bad things we had to deal with. Some Liberians and Sierra Leoneans wanted the opportunity but it never came to pass. Instead, they were drowned to misfortune. Only God knows what happens to them. Some of us are still alive because of God's mercy.

A Guinean Girl

In Guinean, I had to learn the culture. When I first set my eyes on Angeline, I could not resist her friendship. From that day on I knew we liked each other. For Angeline love, I didn't know I would have little problem with her ex-boyfriend. The guy who chose to do his own thing when he could not get his was. It was his girl, but he chose to let go of her and started dating her best friend. When he realized that he had something good, it was too late.

This was not about crimes. If I was arrested it would be about a love affair with a Guinean girl. The guy told lies that I had a love affair with their senior officers' girlfriend instead of a private x-girl-friend. The ex-boyfriend wanted to end my friendship with Angeline. It was late. We both were in love. We wanted to be happy but we had to deal with some difficulties. Where I went to find a safe place had now turned into problem over a love affair. A new battlefield had been established.

The precious life I have been running for God to save in the war was faced with another problem. It was about Angeline who was in love with me. The ex-boyfriend who sought my downfall preferred to use the little dispute of this nature by means of the use of arm. There was no fair trial in this case. The guy only tried to use position or power to settle the matter. I couldn't find a suitable reason why he was coming after me. Angeline was dating this solider- a relationship that lasted for some months. They were no longer boyfriend and girlfriend when I landed in town. What happened? Was he unhappy about my relationship with Angeline when he got the news after few months into our relationship? He wanted her back immediately but to do so, time was needed because she had moved on when their relationship ended. We became best friends and Angeline had my loyal support and respect for her wishes.

According to their neighbors within the vicinity where they both used to live, he did ask her to please consider him as her boyfriend but she refused. She protested that she was in love with me at the time and would not have him back in her life. He was already in a relationship with someone else. She also mentioned it was unfair to treat me that way. Her response became the call for revenge. He was angry and became jealous. His option was to end my relationship Angeline. I was wondering as to what was going on.

When I met Angeline she was single at the time. I made sure the information was correct. Those who knew her also confirmed this information as well. I spoke with one of his best friends who made the matter clear. Their relationship had ended long before my arrival. When I realized he was still interested in Angeline, I met with the guy to have some dialogue. I decided to end my relationship with Angeline if that was what he thought could be the solution. I wanted no problem. On that day, we talked about it and I thought it was over. It would be time consuming to deal with this issue. God also had his own plan for my life. I was vulnerable.

I am friendly and so it worked to my advantage. I was informed that the –ex-boyfriend had other plans. Another struggle had begun because of Angeline. They were determined to accomplish their secret plan against me. This was another setback. I wanted to make the best out of what I had going for me. But love had come my way that I could not easily resist. It was love at first sight. But it would take longer than we had expected for us to meet because we both were busy.

When I first saw Angeline she looked beautiful. Loving Angeline was no crime but the place we chose to love at the time posed many challenges. I was a refugee from Liberia working with the refugees in the camp. Guinean soldiers were popular in town and they were paid in US dollars. They were easy target for the young women as center for attraction for those soldiers. So, going head to head with any Guinean soldier at the time, could be a mistake. It was not my plan or intention to fall out with a Guinean citizen- let alone a soldier over Angeline.

I was out of high school and with my first job, I needed to be careful. Remembering what I was informed about the village, that advice was helpful. Nongoa was a little town. Being in Nongoa town after some months I came across Angeline. When we first met the power of love was in control. We both knew we liked each other on the first day we met. When we had time to meet we became friends. We were determined to have peace in our relationship. Maybe my calculation was poor, but who knows what comes sometime in our lives? Some nights I went to bed awake because I kept thinking about Angeline.

I never knew who she was or her name when I first set eyes on her. I spoke with kids who identified her as Angeline- a student and

Kissi by tribe. It was an advantage for the both of us. We hail from the same tribe, speak the same dialect. Communication would become much easier and even faster when we meet. She spoke French and went to school. I spoke French with her. The French I spoke was not standard. As of that time, I had some information about Angeline. I still had more work to do. My next task was to know where she was living and the kind of connection she had with people in that Town. I had to be mindful and cautious. I didn't want to get drawn into something I really never understood? I did what I had to do to make sure Angeline was single because it was the best thing to do. Had I met her in a relationship, especially with a military guy, it was simple. Walk away from her.

The Guineans had to protect their border because of invading rebel activities. For me, I tried to stay on the safe side and didn't want any conflict with Guinean civilians or soldiers. I made every effort to get the facts before I became best friend with Angeline. That required a lot of time. The information I gathered, was enough to conclude the girl was alone at the time. Her ex-boyfriend who lived next door to her, when I got the news he was her x made it difficult for me to reach Angeline. I wanted to make sure she wasn't hiding anything.

I tried to meet Angeline for the second time since we first met. Three weeks had passed without the chance to see her. I used to dream about her. I knew it would be real. I wanted some answers but I had to wait. On one occasion I saw Angeline walking with a friend to the market. I was there with some of my little friends to purchase food. They knew these soldiers before my arrival in town. As we walked through the market ground, there was Angeline and her friend. On this day I took the time to speak. They all smiled and replied. "We are doing fine." One of my friends interrupted the conversion and said he was a friend of the girls and sometimes went out with them and their boyfriends. It was true. The girls admitted his story was real.

Angeline was free and could talk to the guy of her choice. I wanted to be the one. I even went as far as speaking with Angeline's ex-boyfriend friend. He also told me, "Their relationship ended months even before I came in town." He encouraged me to go after Angeline, if I felt so. I was relief for a moment. Weeks went by without seening Angeline. Unexpectedly, one day on my way to work we ran into each other. I took a deep breath and exhaled some sound of relief.

My likning for Angeline grew even stronger. A breakthrough came for me. My little friend would become the intermediary between Angeline and me. I was wondering when we would meet next to have more time to talk. Things seemed to be working in my favor. More work needed to be done. I had to wait and to finalize every detail or find out everything I wanted to know about her.

After a month and a half I had all the information I needed about Angeline. She was no longer a mystery woman. She was no longer with her x- boyfriend and she wasn't involved with anyone else. I was satisfied with my investigation; it paid off. So it was about time for me to wait to meet Angeline. She was single now and I had nothing to worry about. The next plan was for me to meet with her on neutral ground where I could declare my intention. With the intelligence at my disposal, meeting Angeline took longer than expected. Weeks went by without being able to see her. She had to be in school. Given situation, I needed to wait.

For those who loved someone before, they understand what I am talking about. When two people truly love each other they can do anything just to get closer. I waited for the opportunity to meet with her, so we could talk and get to know ourselves better. One day my plan of meeting Angeline came full circle. Sometimes when I was home from work I used to think about her and when we would meet. Time seemed to be my rival, I thought, but that wasn't the case. I could walk to her house and talk to her because she told my little friend to meet her when I had time. I had to realize one thing. I was warned not to hang around Center town too long because any military men had the right to question anyone at the time, for security reasons. I was informed by some refugees that some people were arrested for these reasons. I was doing everything I could to stay out of trouble. Well-dressed at times could easily get you some attention.

I was young and wanted to look good in front of the girls, but here, I was unable to wear the clothes I had because of attracting atten-tion. This kind of life proved too hard. I felt like one's human rights were being restricted or intimidated. In case of any problem, I had nobody to protect me if everything went wrong for me. The people I met in town were apprehensive because of the huge pressure of mil-itary men deployed in surrounding towns and villages for their own protection. Those who lived in fear were refugees because of their status. I was one of them. For those refugees employed in Guinea, they had to be careful. It made some Guineans jealous because jobs were scarce. If there was any reason to visit center town from the camp, it was to buy food from the market and back. On some days, I used to pass through to go to the other refugee camps to work and back on the camp.

The friends I had were few refugees' boys. I trusted them for many reasons, not all the adults. As refugees we were informed that many Guineans and some refugees were informers for local officials. As refugees, were warned to be careful and to know who to befriend. All the warnings and advices were of more help to me and some

116

refugees. We wanted to live life like a normal people, but we were there to seek refuge. In Nongoa, I used to play soccer with the young men every evening when I left work. Jogging with my dog, Courage, who was my best friend, also helped me along the way.

Angeline lived in town, and if I really wanted to meet her I had to go there. But to do so, somehow meant, being out of the refugee camp. The obstacles were many. Yes, we were in love, but life was the most important thing. I had to put all my fear behind me and follow my heart. I believed it was the right thing to do. In true love there is no fear. Be it darkness or daylight, I was prepared to meet Angeline so we could talk. I was in that position and she also wanted to meet with me. I had waited long enough.

The people I met in town informed me that some refugees had been arrested and nobody heard from them since then. I just didn't know which story to believe anymore. These were frustrating stories for refugees to hear. I was in love and so was Angeline. Nothing could stop true love only God. It would be another crucial experience in that part of Guinea, since fleeing the fighting in Liberia. We wanted to see each other. Food for me, some days was tasteless and my nights very long. It was clear I love to be with the lady on my mind. I had to wait and to take time. There was still more to life and I had to look forward to such times.

Face to Face With Angeline

Angeline had just left her classroom and was on her way home, while I was on my way to work. When I set my eyes on her after almost two months I was astonished and could not find the right words to say to her. I could not believe who was standing in front of me. We were both wishing to meet. There she was standing in my presence.

Having stood there for a while, I said "hi." She also looked into my eyes. From that moment I knew we were falling in love. I was positive she was going to be my girlfriend. She replied and said to me, "how you doing,' using the broken English she learned from some refugees she interacted with. Something funny went on when we met again. Angeline tried to speak to me in English, while I was more interested in speaking the French I learned in high school. We communicated with one another effectively because we spoke the same dialect. Only the pronunciation was different because her speech influenced my French accent and I was influenced by her English accent. I took the lead in the conversation because this was my best shot and I wanted to score the winning goal. "I love you very much and really would like to know you. "I wanted to inform you how much I admire you." She just stood there looking me in the eye and kept smiling. I could see the joy on her face.

She was silent for a while and then, finally, the silence was broken. "She said that she was also thinking about me since we last met in the market,' but she had no clue why she kept feeling that way." From then on I could feel the power of love taking control of us. The big smile on her face just brought comfort and relief. I felt like a huge weight had just been lifted off my body after months of waiting to see her. This was the kind of opportunity I have been waiting on to speak to her one- on -one looking her directly in the eye. So the long waiting day finally came and I was fortunate to face Angeline, as I thought. We made arrangement to meet the next day, but she didn't show up. On the third day I received a message from someone she was going to be my guest. As communication improved between us, so was problem approaching. I did not have the ability to realize what I was getting into. It was incredible that Angeline was coming to pay me a visit. "I can't wait," I told myself many times because my dream was about to come true.

I took some time to clean my house. I decorated and repositioned my room to attract Angeline as I prepared to invite her over. I did everything I could to impress her on our first date. Life in Nongoa town under this unpredictable circumstance because Liberia and Sierra Leone was going through their own troubles, one could only go on a date close to home or take a walk in the refugee camp, or you just had to take a stroll nearby. This could take 45 minutes to the entrance of the town. The shops were small with no space to hang around. Shoppers came and got what they wanted and left. Some just waved to family members and friends.

If I wanted to get something from one of the shops, the best way was to send one of my little friends. They were always around and were familiar with most of the town's people, mostly the military guys on the ground No one paid them any attention or cared to know what they were doing.

I spent most of my time in the camp after work or soccer practice. I was careful because of the scary stories that circulated around town between refugees and the citizens. The people I met in town wore simple cloth even the wealthy ones dressed like the ordinary people. So who was I, not to keep things simple as they were? I had clothes that I felt were casual. They were regular jeans anyone could wear. My life meant more than clothes.

Angeline and I had no walkie–talkie to keep in touch with each other. The only thing I did was to watch and wait. I kept my hopes alive. I expected Angeline anytime.

For sure Angeline appeared like someone who came from the moon and landed on earth. It was a big surprise for me. She had this big smile on her face as she walked closer and closer. Those were some of my happiest moments in life. As she stepped her foot on my front door she was met with a big hug from me. She was happy and relaxed in my arms. She was given a seat and was told to feel at home, which she did with no hesitation. I offered Angeline a drink and something to eat

Music was also available for her entertainment. Few of my little friends were there. It was a special moment for us; we celebrated together. For the time being, I knew the hard work was over and it was time to sit and talk with Angeline. We were getting along well.

I didn't know that her ex-boyfriend wanted her back. His intention to have her back created another problem. After the news of my love affairs with Angeline, Some believed she still had some connection with the ex-boyfriend. I took my time to ask those around and waited to make sure. It was then that we started to talk. It was confirmed they were no longer together. We all lived in the same town so I made sure it was true. Angeline and I had created a bond when we met on that wonderful day. We made love. It was one of the finest moments for lovers. I will never forget how it felt having her in my arms.

Our bond grew strong and we worked to sustain a relationship. We were now exposed and many people knew we were dating. The news quickly spread like a wild fire. It was real and we could not deny the fact. I was in love and so was Angeline. However, something would keep us apart from seeing each other for a while. It was one of those difficult times we had to cope with for being lovers in such times. I was hunted by Angeline's ex-boyfriend and few of his friends because of Angeline. She was deeply concerned and worried about my safety. Angeline wasn't their target. The target, getting me out of the way would once again secure his return.

The battle was tough for me. It was like the cold war between the Soviet Union and the United States. The ex-boyfriend was moving slowly toward me, and his intention was destruction. This I knew for sure. My loyal friends told me how deadly his plan had turned to get me.

The table was turning against me. The happy times I had in Nongoa town were about to come to an end. Life was heading in the wrong direction. The peace of mind I had invested in was out of the box. I trusted no one again except my little friends as my informants. The threat was serious and I had to be careful and going back to the old ways of life during the civil war, was the last thing I wanted to return to again. Nevertheless, it was late to reverse the circumstances.

I created my own circumstances and we were exercising our right to love and to be loved. So, to those who were coming after me, had no idea of this basic right. The only way to pay for my wrongdoing if there was any for Angeline's ex- boyfriend to be happy was to do so with my life. Such sacrifice was insane.

I had no choice, but to pray. I was in a big mess. I mean, bigger than I imagined. My life was about to be taken away. I had to put my trust in the Lord for my rescue. The enemies were many and powerful. I was a single guy with no weapon to defend myself against them. My little friends were the loyal ones I had left. I explained to my friends what I expected of them. I was leaving them because Angeline and I became friends when we met while she was single.

They were coming after me as fast as they could. The kids wanted to do everything to help me out. The same kids also ran errands for Angeline's ex-boyfriend and some of his friends in town and some on the camp. I was blessed with a flow of steady information reaching me on a daily basis.

The kids were more committed to me since they understood the threat made on my life. I am grateful to God for them. I was also there for them when they needed me as well. I became their friend from the day I met them. I had the instinct to identify with their plight as refugees. I was one of them. The difference between these kids and as me was that I was out of high school and with a job. I was earning some money and the kids needed some assistance. I fully understood what it meant to be a refugee–no support from anyone or family member. The day I met them I accepted them with no question. Who am I to question God's creation? They are the best experience I like to adore and to cherish in my lifetime. I was once in their shoes when I first set foot on Guinea territory and as times went by they kept bringing other friends.

Life in Nongoa, as rebels in Sierra Leone fought government troop, was risky for refugees. Those kids were like my guardian angels. The children went out of their way to make sure I knew who my enemies were, and which part of town they resided, because of their loyal support, I had the opportunity to know which way to go and whom to keep an eye on. I had not given up on my faith in God. He alone could make a way out for me.

The Guinean soldiers were many in town. It was impossible to recognize the ones who were on the hunt for me. Their plan against me was Angeline's soldier ex-boyfriend idea of revenge. The Guinean Government had no part in this.

I needed an organized and loyal circle of friends. Those were my little friends from the refugee camp. I knew I could trust them. We had cooked, shopped and hanged together. Their parents knew me well and were satisfied with that friendship. I had also helped them with their homework. I also helped with other contributions. We had established a bond no one could easily destroy. They had confidence in me and they understood we were true friends. We became a family tree that no one could break. Our bonds were guaranteed and full of love.

My friends understood that my life was at stake. If I ever needed them, this was the time. It was impossible to sleep at night. Some of the Guinean soldiers had turned their honor into personal revenge. Even their own citizens were afraid of them. They looked fearful in their uniforms, especially when they were back from duty. These were men in arms, trained to fight and to kill. I was nothing to guys coming after me but a little rat very easy to step on and get done with, within seconds.

I had no family member, in Nongoa Town, which meant I had to be very careful. The plot at first seemed not too serious to me. I only realized when news of three missing guys started circulating around town. One of them was a refugee teacher from Sierra Leone.

Days after their disappearance, news arrived that he had been tortured beyond recognition. His killers used a knife to cut his body up. His body was buried under sand leaving his head above the sand. He was left there to die slowly, leaving his poor wife to look after the kids. How true this information was, I don't know? I was new in that area. But the news by itself was terrifying and the event very sad. It left the refugees, including me, in deep fear.

If a teacher was arrested and disappeared for good it was clear, no one was safe. Since I was new in town I was an easy target for them. The plot to hunt me down was very serious and not to be overlooked. I didn't know who would be the next refugee on their list. It was sad the poor teacher was dead and gone.

According to some of the people I interviewed in that town, the teacher had had an affair with the wife of a Guinean citizen. The enemies' solution was brute force. I was there to know about this. We were refugees and our rights did not make any difference.

One day I decided to pay Angeline a visit at her parent's house where she lived. Many days went by without seeing her. I feared she too was under surveillance. Leaving the camp to find Angeline would be a terrible error.

I spent most of my time on the camp. What in the world got into my head to make such a move on that day? What was I thinking? I was to provide my own answer. I left the camp and stepped foot in danger zone. Few yards away from Angeline's house, it felt like something had gotten hold on me. I was frozen for about ten minutes a sense of cold rushed through my body. My feet became so heavy under me. It felt like the whole world was about to crumble on top of me.

I haven't felt this way since I escaped the fighting in my own home country, Liberia. The message was clear that I was in serious danger. This was not the only sign or indication that I was on the verge of falling. All my dreams were about to die along with me. Dreams were going to be dead; I could tell that it was not God's approval but choices and poor judgments I made.

It was about time to pay the price for my decisions. I took a few steps and then, took a deep breath. I told one of my accompanied little friends that I was in danger. I had to be very mindful of my movement around town. He acknowledged he saw fear in my eyes. He was deeply worried and troubled.

On my way to see Angeline I saw signs of trouble ahead. I approached the building where Angeline and her family lived; I came face to face with her Military boyfriend. I was already there so there was no chance to hide from him. He was cleaning his AK47. I was not afraid because he had AK 47; I saw different types of revolvers in the Civil War. Even though I hated being around guns I learned from watching other kids my age that fought alongside different warring factions carried them. When our eyes met I saw the jealousy in his face. His body and face took a different shape. His face changed and his eyes grew cold and deep. Even though I was worried, I spoke to him in French, as a sign of respect. It is just a normal way of life in Africa. So no matter how bitter he was, I owed him his respect. I was much younger than he was and it was the right thing to do and greeting him would not resolve the dispute between us over Angeline. He was still bitter, even far more so because I was there to visit her. He suspected she was in love with a refugee boy from Liberia. His friend told me they were no longer together. I noticed that for months.

When I noticed he still loved her, I decided to keep away from Angeline. He was still mad and I didn't know why. His aim was clear towards me. In such predicament, I tried to negotiate. He said it was fine at first, and he even told one of my little friends too.

He gathered few sympathizers on his side to help him and I still noticed he was still not happy. He was backed by support from some of his friends. They could back him in case of anything. That was the way I thought.

The refuges were at times happy, but they wanted to go back home. They were vulnerable inhabitants in that part of Africa. Africa which was once held high as a peaceful continent had turned into refugee camps.

My decision to venture from my safety zone in search of Angeline was the start of renewed trouble in civil war. It left me vulnerable once again. My heart was never at peace again. I thought of many things now.

I had no doubt about his plan to take revenge. I was now with the young woman he realized was gone. Arresting me, I thought at the time was on his mind. The crisis over Angeline, could have led to my downfall. On my way to Angeline's house, I had bought some food for us. What I did not realize was that my plans for that day was about to changed.

I tried to open the beef can but I broke the attached key to the can, and so, I found another way to open it. The only option was to use a knife. This too was risky and with the knife, I missed the can, and the knife went through the fingers of my left hand. I bled for the rest of that evening. We did everything we could to do to stop the bleeding, but we could do so completely. Angeline even tore her lapper and tied my finger just to prevent the flow of blood.

From that moment on I knew that the plot was serious. I began to double down my activities there. My body slowed down. I lost a lot of blood. I had to leave. I was too close or directly in the enemy territory. As nightfall approached, I decided to leave and return to the camp.

I immediately went to my room and got on my knees, asking the Lord to show me mercy in the midst of my trouble. I could not sleep for fear of what would happen to me. I cried deeply from the bottom of my heart. I was nervous as to my fate in a foreign country.

I had no way of knowing I would see Angeline again, given my painful experience there. But she walked a mile under thick cloud of darkness to check on my progress. This is true love. Fearing nothing, she came under the dark. I was tired but excited to see her, especially coming at that time of the night. It rained heavily that night, the sky was very dark. It was cold as well and I wasn't expecting any visitor. True love is something no one can take away.

When I saw her I also felt a sense of relief, but I knew my life was on the line for falling in love. Angeline tied my finger; but my blood still ran down my finger and with no good hospital near or far, it became a problem.

The entire town became a place of terror that I could not easily venture out in the streets; I felt now I was a wanted person. The enemies were not coming after her. I was their target. Their plan to murder me was now at their pleasure.

When Angeline sat on my bed, I struggled to squeeze few words out of my mouth. I asked why she took such a risk to come to my aid.

She spoke bravely. If anything had happened so be it. I love you and I am not staying away from you, no matter what. I will be around you. I love you. Why I can't see you? Fear is not going to prevent me from seeing you.

Angeline never fully understood the gravity of the risk that had me and how it was affecting my progress. Angeline's stand point, love was a free gift from above and so we had the right to love each other if that was the way we felt. I felt that too, especially from the beginning, but now it was a bit scary. She lacked the mind to understand that different people do things differently for various reasons. The enemies had the power to harm us. I was seeing far beyond Angeline. That night she gave me a bath. I stood there like a baby receiving a bath from mother.

She reminded me of my mother I left in Liberia. I was going to spend more years without seeing her. However, in this moment and time, Angeline was the woman in my life and my attention was all focused on her and the direction in which our relationship was going.

The Lord Made a Way

How and when God made a way for me to leave Nongoa is unclear because of my state of mind at the time. However, I can still remember the months which lead up to the event, and the whole drama of me being wanted dead or alive. The reason I had to leave Nongoa the way I did was for loving someone. I was in love with a Guinean girl.

The year was 1998 and the months were October, November and December, when almost the entire world was anticipating the biggest season of the year Christmas. Like millions around the world, I was excited for the Christmas celebration. I wanted to spend it with the love of my life and my family in the District of Gueckedou. Everything I had planned was mere illusion by this time. Here, I was dying for some form of protection from the very people who were supposed to protect the town's people. I was still alive, but it felt as if I was dead from the inside. I only traveled with an empty body.

Sleepless nights, lack of appetite, desperation, insecurity and worst of all, loneliness, were the common human phenomenon I had to deal with in that environment. I had no one else to really count on except God and my little friends I had with me. The children were loyal and brought information to me about the traitors. What they could not do was to get me out of enemy zone.

Leaving the enemy zone was my priority and nothing more than that. I had no choice, but to leave. The news of my attempted arrest spread around town but none came up to say anything to me about what was under way. I concluded that my enemies were many and that they knew about a plot against me. I wanted to know who these elements were, especially those on the civilian side of the plot.

The task of leaving Nongoa proved crucial; I could not do it alone. I needed assistance to accomplish this adventure. I took some time to rethink my plans and to find whether that was possible. For days and weeks I tried to come up with a plan to deal with the task. My only hope was for God's guidance and timely intervention.

The Lord, whose power and miracles are far beyond man understands, answered my prayers and exposed my enemies in broad daylight as I expected. While I was in bed and fast asleep, the Lord revealed my enemies to me. In my dream, they were seated around a table discussing their plan to take my life from me. I saw their faces very clearly and recognized each and every one of them, down to the color of clothes they wore. The good thing about this dream was that my enemies discussed their clandestine plan in detail.

It seemed impossible that my boss was the leading speaker among these conspirators planning to murder an innocent person. Everything was clear and all too real to deny.

In my dream, my dog Courage, was with me as we walked through the refugee camp and were few steps away from my boss's house. I could see my plotters from where I walked with my dog. When they saw me, they laughed as if it was something funny. I took a few steps almost passing my boss's house I turned my head to my right to look back. I saw him pointing his finger behind my back. My boss was selling me out. He was selling me. He was betraying me.

His actions reminded me of the story of Jesus and Judas. The one who knew me so well betrayed me. He had released important information to those who wanted to capture me. When our eyes met, I knew from that day he was the key plotter in the conspiracy. Everything happened in my dream.

Waking up the next morning, I was horrified and dismayed about what I had witnessed. I had been warned that my enemies were doing everything to murder me. I could not ignore that dream; it was all too real. I was in danger of was losing my life, not in a cat and mouse game, but in a love game. As Bob Marley once said, "Your worst enemy could be your best friend and your best friend your worst enemy." So my boss, whom I once thought had my back, had become a different person. I was still curious to confirm what I saw in my dream.

The Lord was about to expose my enemies to me in broad daylight, once and for all, as it had been in my dream. Was this not a miracle of God, the Creator of the Universe? I gave thanks to God for this dream. It became a major factor in my safe escape from that town.

It was a breakthrough for me because of the mercy of the Lord. My enemies knew exactly what they were looking for and who they were looking for. Having being put on alert that their hunt for me had intensified, I changed my location every night. To conceal my plans for the night, I spent most of my free time during the day after work or soccer practice, just to convince my slayers I was home and was not going anywhere.

My way of life had changed because my boss had given my enemies they information they needed to end my life. He knew almost everything about me-my family connection, friends and where I could be found. He was a major threat to me and I had to be careful. I had to remain alert, focus and mindful.

I was deeply worried and frightened. The truth was I couldn't do much to undo what was happening. I needed to stay away from Angeline. It was too late to stop my enemies from attempting to carry out what they had already planned against me. I had no one else on my side but God, and my little friends. The children did their best to keep me informed on a daily basis, but their information was not enough to save me. Something urgent needed to be done. If I were to survive I had to think clear.

It was difficult, spending the night home by myself. I didn't trust those guys an inch. Finding a different location to spend my nights I was only part of the solution to my problem. Whose house was safe for me to spend the nights away from the comfort of my home and bed? Who knew whether someone in the house where I thought was safe might not be an informer waiting there?

I thought up a plan to find some classmates who lived on the refugee camp. The next thing was to find which area of the camp my classmates live in. On the other hand, I had to be discreet in explaining my situation to all my classmate friends, for fear some could betray me.

As someone who once lived in war torn countries, using human intelligence was part of my strategy. The friends I selected to spend some night with were those I could count on. Every night, I sneaked out of my house just to be safe. The dark was the perfect time to hide from my enemies. They were armed so I had to be careful.

My dog's job was to spend his nights outside, to ensure that no one trespassed on the local property of the government where I lived. He did his job well and was well fed every day. On rainy nights, he was taken inside to enjoy the warmth of the house. Sleeping with friends became another issue, we avoided the use of candlelight, or any form of light.

I was taking a huge risk but that was the only thing I could think of doing. In the morning, I left early, using different routes, and making sure no one knew where I slept or was coming from. This kind of life was like a thorn in my flesh. The cold, droplets of water from leaves and trees, the restless night, the fear that someone could end my life anytime, seemed too real to cope with.

My friends were loyal to the end and they never betrayed me during this dangerous period of my life, since time was not in my favor. Every passing day was crucial.

To take a safe path from the town that was no longer secure, I used the local NGO's car which brought workers to the camp. Using commercial vehicles would have been a mistake because these vehicles were subjected to inspection at every checkpoint.

Another important consideration during this period was time. Leaving assigned areas while still on duty, without permission, meant no pay, and could be followed by dismissal. I loved my job and wanted to maintain it for the time being. My priority was working for those living at the mercy of God. I didn't want to distance myself from their plight. I was one of them and fully understood what it was walking in their shoes, and experiencing their everyday maneuvers to survival.

Leaving them behind to me was a setback in my pursuit, as a caring social worker, of the ethics of the profession. This was my conviction, but my life was at stake, and I believed it was smart to leave that town and live to work another day. That was the only way out.

The enemies would never give up no matter what. These guys were determined to carry out their evil plans. They had the government on their side. They were well armed. I was vulnerable and powerless.

Angeline would not be able to help me in this fight. She was totally unaware and was unable to see the seriousness of my fate. The school year was coming to an end and students were in high spirit for the Christmas break. The upcoming vacation meant Angeline had to leave for the big town. She would have to leave alone. Her departure would bring some relief to me, and would ease the tension among the aggressors and their plan. That was what I thought.

But Angeline's absence increased the threat made on my life. It was clear to the enemies Angeline would not have left town without some agreement between us. They were right on that point. However, I did not have the will to stop her from leaving. We both lived in the same town, but couldn't see each other in this critical time. It brought too much frustration on us, and a huge blanket of fear.

My life was in chaos. It was proper for her to leave me behind and spend time with her mother. I had plans to leave any way. What kept holding me back was the means to do so safely. October had ended, and we were now in November, with only a month left for the Christmas celebration. I was anxious every minute, every second, and hour that passed by.

One can imagine how tough and hopeless life seemed at the time.

Before Angeline's departure we met for the last time to say goodbye. As a man, I concealed my fears to accommodate hers. We spoke for a while and I told her to leave. She was very anger and questioned me for going against her will. She was the love of my life, but our safety and happiness was under threat.

I had to put my fleshly desires aside and see clearly what the future held for me. She was driven by emotions and passion to be loved. She accused me of being insecure. That was her point of view and state of mind. What about my life that was on the line combined with the struggle to eat and to sleep every night I spent in the area? Angeline could not see the problem I saw at the time.

Was she was a little selfish at the time, putting her needs before my safety? Nothing at this moment seemed to make sense to either of us. Looking back, I have learned from the past and hope to grow on a day- to- day basis. It was a typical innocent love story with many conditions attached to it. A relationship that has no solid foundation cannot last.

It was the blind leading the blind. We were devastated, angry, and left with no real sense of purpose in our relationship.

It seemed loving Angeline had happened at a bad time. It was the wrong time and the wrong place.

My desire to love and be with Angeline had to slow down. I had to step aside for the sake of our lives. Her departure brought me more threats, but it was the right step. I put some things together for Angeline to take with her for her mother, a gift from someone Angeline's mother had not set her eyes on yet. She packed up and left for town. She stood in tears and a heart broken. These are sacrifices made when you love someone at some point in life. I was hurt and confused when she left, but life went on. I was left on alone but God was on my side. So we still had hope and we weren't giving in to the enemy's demand

I was in love with Angeline and wanted to be close to her. I had to face the fact she was now nowhere to be seen. The lonely days and nights felt too long to handle alone. Half of me was gone with little hope that we would see each other again. I can't accurately describe what was going through my mind or head. There is a saying that "he who feels it knows it." The load seemed too heavy to hold on to.

December came and the hunt to capture me kept on. The bad men showed no sign of retreating. I managed to get by on a daily basis, but with less enthusiasm on the job and life. I was falling apart rapidly. My sickness was one doctors couldn't diagnose. The only cure would be to have Angeline back in my life, but not now.

When Angeline left Nongoa, the news of her departure quickly spread around town. I was surprised by what some had to say to me about her. I admit I knew about her plan to leave for vacation. What was clear was that I had no power to stop her. Like me, she was filled with regrets and emptiness. There was no progress for us in an environment filled with men in arms. They had been brought there to protect their border from neighboring unrest. The commanders on my case, and their men decided to change the rules of engagement on ground.

These men had different motive. Those hunting me, I thought, were no longer our protectors if they were in the first place. Their plan was changed to suit their own agenda. It was not a good thing. We wanted the fighting to stop so we could return to our respective countries.

Many were threatened by their presence on the camp. I was saddened to learn of the way the ex-boyfriend made open threats against my life.

I was exposed to their plan and the evil they harbored against me. In life there is always a price to pay for the choices we make. I was worried and inwardly felt sick.

My enemies boasted how they were going to inflict pain on me after my capture. If they thought I was guilty, a fair trial should have taken place. But they had no case against me and if my crime was to love Angeline, I had yet to wait for a government in Guinea that would indict a man for loving someone single when I met her.

The woman in question had left–long gone. I was still with them. I was outnumbered and a slim chance of escaping was equally challenging. Angeline was someone I met alone. She had no boyfriend when we met. She was single and her ex-boyfriend had another girl.

I dreamed almost every night about Angeline, and how happy we had been. It was so heartbreaking the next morning, waking up to find myself still wanted if anyone who could find me.

I was still determined to continue to wait on God to make a way for my escape. I had not given up faith and hope in God. He was my source of courage in weakness. He fought my would be assassins and brought me out of the shadow of death.

By December, I remained to wait for an NGO car to get me out of Nongoa as soon as possible. I felt how close I was to being captured alive. Feeling of death threat is real once you live through it and survive. On a bright sunny day, while we were at work, our director arrived with a three month salary for all employees. Everyone was happy and anticipated leaving for the Christmas holiday. I seemed happy, but inside, I prayed only to leave the town. The feeling that I was surrendered by enemies kept reoccurring again and again. It was time to leave no matter what.

The night before arrival of our organization's director, I parked my belongings in the middle of the night. I cannot recall where the energy came from, but it came handy. I told friends it was time to leave. It was a tough decision to make. I had no choice or any other way to settle my issues with those who wanted me dead. If I wanted to live to see another day this was the safest passage, the Lord had planned for me.

My friends were informed of my plan to leave the next morning, or the following day. I asked them not to reveal my plan. They were loyal and did exactly what I told them. I gathered few of my belongings and gave each one some of my things I felt would help them through those difficult times.

I was nervous, desperate and didn't know whether I would see them again. It was very hard to look them in the eye and lie to them that I was coming back soon. I took a deep breath and looked around I knew I wasn't coming back to stay but hope to pass through to go to work.

I was aware of the impact my untimely departure would have on the minds of my little friends I was ready to leave behind. These were friends who were loyal to me, and had never betrayed me. Here, I was leaving them not certain about the future and what it would be for them. I was also aware of their parent's situation. They could not afford to provide these kids with the basic needs in life. I had tried to be there for them and to share everything to improve their wellbeing. I was not a rich man, but I had a job. I felt guilty I was leaving them, but it was a matter of life and death. These children couldn't provide for themselves. They lived in depravation in a refugee camp.

Some brought wood on their heads in market grounds in exchange for a few pennies to buy food. Many did not want to pay for wood when they could get it for themselves.

Their parents brought home little portion of food to keep families going. The UN tried its best to feed thousands of refugees but it wasn't enough for many thousands more.

UN rations were giving on a monthly basis, barely enough to sustain them for a long time. They were fed Bugler wheat and corn meal. This was a struggle for survival. The bugler wheat was strange for these refugees whose staple food was rice. The change in their diet led many to get sick. The bugler wheat in the form of rice, harvested on the farm had to be ground to suit their taste. By the time that process was over, half the bag of wheat was gone.

How anyone expected ration of this sort to last long for a family of four or more. Their plight seemed doomed. Hope for them seemed a distant future. They were destitute and some seemed willing to give up on life. I was well informed of their situation and as it difficult; life at the time seemed hopeless. They were subjected to hardship, neglected, and left to answer their own question about life or death. No matter how much assistance refugees received from NGO's, it could not substitute for the losses and senseless suffering. They had lost their human dignity and confidence. What more can be said about this unfortunate circumstances, or which words can be used to describe how destructive war can be?

I wished I had the power to change the situation on the ground, and enjoy the friendship I established with my friends on the refugee camps. They were heroes who wanted the best for me. They helped to save my life. Here, I was running away, and was leaving them in the same mess I met them in. With their bravery and endless sacrifices and with God's help, I emerged victorious from the war. Their courage to survival among Guineans as refugees became the tool which paved a planned escape from Nongoa town.

In the book, "The Shallow Graves of Rwanda, written by Shaharyar. Khan, who served as the UN Secretary-General's Special Representative in Rwanda, reminded me of the civil war in Liberia.

The entire world had witnessed one of the fastest destruction of human lives carried out in history, which came to be known as "The Rwandan Genocide."

Khan gives detail account of a twelve year old Hutu girl he named, "Sainte" Helen'. This story is exceptional and deserves some international recognition for its brilliance in a timely intervention for a teenage girl, who saved innocent lives, lives already marked to be butchered.

Helen played with three kids who came from a Tutsi family in the same neighborhood in Rwanda before the Genocide. At the peak the elders had limited time to hide a woman and her four children in the attic. The elders never survived in their good intentions to protect family members from danger. They were chopped into pieces, and their bodies thrown in a mass grave.

Few days passed by with no food or water for them to drink. The mother couldn't live to see the children starve to death. She died to save lives when she made the decision to leave the attic and creep down to prepare food for the children before her killers developed suspicion that people were in the building.

The scent quickly spread, reaching the neighbors. She was betrayed by some of the neighbors. Upon receiving the information the killers wasted no time to move in and finish their victim, while the little ones watched in fear and in disbelief.

Critical aspect of this story, as of today, remains a mystery, not only in my view, but many of Khan's readers who would agree with me. How did Helen instantly realize her friends were in the attic? It was divine intervention of God.

Helen took food secretly to the house where her friend's mother had been brutally murdered. She went back the next day but the bowl was empty. Helen knew her little friends were still alive and needed more food to sustain them. She brought food every evening, place the food at the same location as she did the previous day. Helen's family was forced to leave their home in Rwanda for the jungle or forest of Congo, to escape the Tutsi dominance in Rwanda after they succeeded in driving out the Hutus fighters.

The night before she left with her parents, Helen made her final visit with another bowl of food, leaving it at the exact spot like the rest of the time; she knelt down and prayed, said her goodbye, well in her heart and was gone. God answered her prayers.

The children were later discovered when the {RPF} forces took control of the city and searched the building. The children were adopted by their Aunts who came from abroad to search for them. Khan never met the hero he named "Sainte Helen." According to Khan, "Helen was twelve when he served in Rwanda, in 1990. His book on Rwanda was released in 2000. Helen by this time, if still alive, is in her twenties.

Helen hasn't, received any award or recognition for her extraordinary initiative, leadership and courage.

That is why children are supposed to be cherished. Like Helen, my little friends at Nongoa were brave and compassionate. Helen is similar to my angels on earth, for those lamenting periods of my life. I was leaving them behind, but my heart remained with them. Who would replace me, which was my major concerned?

I would almost sacrifice every penny I own to see them smile. Everything was coming to an end and would soon become something of the past.

Receiving three months of salary, it I felt was the best time to leave. I shared most of my things with my friends and left them money to buy food. I left my dog behind, too. That was frustrating and difficult. He was nervous and confused but I provided money for his up- keep. I hoped to come back to get him but I wasn't too sure of that either.

I was packed and ready to go. I eagerly awaited the next NGO vehicle. Our bosses arrived with our salaries, but left to go to another camp.

The enemies had set traps for me and their informers increased in size, also. There was nowhere to hide, as every move was observed in the camps, around town, and not too far from the house where I lived. My way out was the NGO's vehicle.

The American Refugee committee vehicle entered the camp with one of their workers to do some quick assessment and return to Gueckedou. This was the opportunity I had been praying and wishing for. It came at the best time for my departure from Nongoa. I could not afford to lose the only chance that the Lord had provided for me.

Immediately, I went ahead to negotiate plans for my departure. The driver immediately instructed his associate to take me with them. I was asked to bring my things hastily on board. "Yes, I said. The arrangement was finalized and we took off.

My freedom seemed closer than I thought. I was about to experience a new beginning in my life once more. Fear, loneliness, sleepless nights, and the lack of appetite were about to come to an end. A new beginning was approaching. Peace with myself was more important for me.

Our departure brought great relief. I took a deep breath of peace. I sat in the four-wheel jeep to Guckedou. God knew what in the world was going through my head as the driver put his foot on the accelerator. My body brought back the kind of hope I could not describe.

It has been such a long time since I had such extraordinary peace; my ordeal begun some four months ago. We drove through the camp as I looked back at our office building. The green grass surrounding the soccer field, where I played with boys in the town, seemed too real to ignore.

I was on my way to safety; and a new journey had commenced for me. I felt renewed in strength and I was taking with me memories of families and friends I met in Nongoa. We approached the security checkpoint, my heart pounded and fear creped in I thought I would be order to step out of the vehicle. I prayed. I was blessed we were allowed to go through the checkpoint. The guards at the check point spoke politely and signaled us to go through. I was thankful to God for his grace and mercy as we strolled through carefully.

The journey was about an hour and we were at the last check-point to enter Gueckedou. This time, I did not panic; we were only five minutes away from town. I was confident everything was going well. Sure, we made it safely in town where the mood was different.

Here, many people walked the main street, through the market ground. Buyers and sellers alike came from different directions. I was fascinated and satisfied I was back in town to see my family and meet with loved ones.

Meeting Angeline now was my priority. She was eagerly awaiting my arrival as well. In Gueckedou, we had the freedom to be together and do the things we wanted to do. My fear went away, but not completely. I had a second thought on mind. I was aware that my rights as a refugee were also limited; I had watched my back continually. I knew I was out of the enemy town, but I was only an hour's drive away. They could reach me if they chose to do so. They had the will and means to come after me.

143

They were respected in every part of the country and I was still a refugee. I could have been arrested even though there would have been no proof of any misdeeds. I was more concerned to meet Angeline and my family. What I did not know all this time was that the news of my problems had already began making headlines in town, especially in my family.

The table had turned for me. I was home to meet my family, who anxiously awaited my arrival. I was held in high esteem for my bravery because God was on my side.

I listened attentively as Uncle and his wife stated their points about my failure to pay heed to the warning I had been given at the start of the civil war. I had long regretted my action and had asked the Lord to forgive me. While it was true my parents were upset, they were happy to see me alive and home with them. I wanted to see Angeline. We met and everyone was happy to be at ease. On my way to Angeline, I asked a few friends and neighbors to accompany me.

I met Angeline; there were hugs and the kisses. The silence was broken, and broken hearts were mended. Everything went fine. I was introduced to my mother in-law for the first time. It was a joyous day for all.

She blamed herself for not being there when the race began. I could see in my mother in-law's eyes how happy she was to have her daughter around. Everything went good and life went on as we all went about doing what we wanted to do in life.

Angeline complained that her former boyfriend was having an affair with her best friend and his action only tarnished her relationship with her friend.

He had been bothered by Angeline's decision to walk away from him. My arrival and encounter with Angeline was the trigger that made him want Angeline back.

I had no part to play in their separation. I was the scapegoat: I arrived long after they separated. Angeline and her best friend look almost alike in appearance. They both had light skinned in complexion, about the same height, and were classmates.

One can only imagine how she felt in coping with the fact that her soldier boyfriend was in love with her best friend. My arrival in Nongoa town marked a new beginning in Angeline's life. It brought some happiness.

She was pleased when we met. I treated her with respect and affection. It helped to regain her confidence. She was proud being with me. I was much younger, just coming out of high school, with a job. The future, from her perspective, seemed promising. The only missing piece was we both still had to focus on our goals.

I happened to be the youngest social worker at the time on ground. I was new in town. Beautiful girls and women were saying hi with such big smiles on their faces.

I was mindful not to chase after girls. I was in love with Angeline from the very day I set eyes on her. But I had to wait. We had some good times together; it lasted for a while and we went our separate ways. I had to return to Liberia because of the attacks by rebels loyal to former Liberian rebel leader, Charles Taylor in that part of Guinea where I lived.

Angeline went back to the very town where we met to continue her education and be with her dad. The lessons I learned from my past would help me in making good decision in the future.

Now, looking back on those times in my life and family, I believe life will be better soon. But the truth is, there are millions of people in the world whose problems might be even worse than what my family and I went through.

The Liberian Civil War landed me in Guinea as a refugee, barely managing to stay alive. I had to be patient to wait on God's time throughout my journey to ease stresses, and without the help of God, I couldn't have made it in those times, or even now. I need him every step of the way.

Liberians blamed the civil war on politicians and military leaders for the mass unrest they created on the people of Liberia, especially the young generation. We shouldn't ignore the fact that many Liberians were not innocent in a war they helped to bring on themselves. We thought we wanted a quick fix to our political problems. We are left with regrets because some supported a cause we did not understand out to help. It would be fear that those who supported the war; for one reason or the other to share in taking some blames.

To move ahead as a people and as a nation, we should ask God to forgive us as we seek to forgive ourselves, and also as we forgive those who took the lives of our love ones.

We had another option to settle our differences, but some chose to plunge our country in a senseless blood bath. The War nearly rendered us hopelessly hopeless; together we will still prevail as a people. All we can do now is to pull what best remains in us in order to gain our self- respect and national dignity.

A Revelation

"**B**orn with a Vision*"* became the final resolution! It was a wakeup call. A call no one in my family was prepared to answer, but it was a call for a greater purpose. Someone had to answer this call, but whom? We needed to distinguish the right voice. There were many voices calling from complete darkness. We wanted to hear a voice in the light. It would take longer than expected to recognize the voice of truth. It became two wars in one man's mind to search for his family trapped in a nasty civil war, or to follow his destiny. It was a choice he had no control over. Walk in the mind of the author and the long awaited vision.

"Born with a Vision" was never possible, had it not been for some sort of divine intervention -a vision darkness tried to delay. Where was the light? How could anyone believe then that the fight against long suffering and hardship would come to an end? The longing for peace and stability which had disappeared from the family, was long overdue —something we had desperately yearned for, for so long. How long was it to last to have this very important human desire come true? Will the entire family meet a premature death before there

can be any change for the better, or who in the family will live to tell the story? Many are call, but few are chosen.

A spiritual battle had begun many years ago. The enemy's aim was not just at destroying the physical body of each member in the family, they were determined to crush the spirit, the only force that keeps the human going, even when it seems that hope is a distance away. It was a war we never had any chance to win on our own. It took the almighty God to give us victory. It was the kind of force no human could accurately comprehend. This was God's family and he was now part of us. How could anyone escape this circle of misfortunes hunting the family? Years went by and the parents whose shoulders the family depended on were dead and gone. Few of his siblings were also forced to their early grave before the secret was revealed. Our questions for years had to be answered by God who is beyond our human comprehension. He was the only power capable of exposing the forces behind the witch hunts that penetrated the very core of the family. Constant attacks shattered some of the happiest times in our union.

For divine reasons, and at some point in time, the evil that sought to tear our livelihood apart had to come to an end. Was it too late form a human stand point? The unpredictable years of separation by distance, and the conditions that lasted had left scars on the minds of those who had survived the carnage in the civil war. How to get out of the destruction was not just a physical condition, but equally a spiritual factor –an all-out war waged against the family. It became clear to me that those who see the future through the eyes of love, are like Daniel in the lion's den, still seeing the light even when there seems to be no sign of life. We believed.

It turns out that these were times that we needed a divine solution. As a family, we could not define our complex and degrading circumstances, mostly prolonged by the Liberian Civil War. Entangled by grieve, and his absence from the family, the writer stood in the center of the field of green grass, thinking about the miseries in Life. It was too much to bear as a teen, transitioning into adulthood. It was like being in the middle of nowhere. Standing still, and lost in his thoughts, it felt like consulting his Creator about what was ahead. He was not sure at the time what to expect.

He was now face- to -face with the reality of his family's nightmare. With ten years gone by, no means to contact his family, and not knowing their where about, made everything around him hopeless. He was now confronted with his future that was at stake. He imagined himself far away from his entire body. In a lonely world, his meditation was not recognized by the deepness of life, he envisioned his presence somewhere out there. Not knowing where, surrounded by six other continents, he is standing on one foot still learning to walk on both feet. He needed a vision. It was already taking shape, but he was too immature to understand. His body, standing there, seemed he was out of it. He wondered what life could be like out there in the big world.

His home country was not safe to return. Where else could he find rest? It would take many challenging and bitter years to share the extraordinary story of an ordinary family's resilience effort to stay alive in midst of a deviant storm. Those lost years were the darkest period of his family's life. What could be done? It was an uncertain journey with no flexibility for surrendered. Triumph had to be the only way out for righteousness to conquer evil. Now, here comes this thrilling story of how the weakest are becoming the strongest by faith. It is a story that will leave your heart melting and would stare something on the inside for you, too, to rise above your obstacles. It can be. A vision became the only way out.

On the center of the world's stage his vision was threatened by the same forces he thought he had left behind. There was no other option. All he had left was his faith. Patiently, he waited in expectation.

"Born with a Vision" is not a one man's vision. It is one man, walking in the shoes of billions around the world. It is our vision for a better world. Don't wait to be told about Your vision. You are a part of that vision. It is Your vision. Your vision is not something you are separated from. In fact; it is your purpose on this earth. Will you find it?

References

Dallaire, Romeo; (2003). Shake Hands With The Devil. Canada, Random House Ca.

Khan, S. M. (2000). *The shallow graves of rwanda*. New York, NY: I. B. Taurus Publishers.

Nehsahn P. Z. M. (2006). *The power of caring An everyday devotional* Enumclaw, WA: Pleasant Word.

Samura, S. (2010). Cry freetown. Retrieved from http://www.cryfree-town.org/ Verses marked NIV taken from the New International Version Bible, 1973, 1978, 1984 by International Bible Society. Takirambudde, P. (2002, Novermber 25. Guinea: Security of Liberian refugees [online news blog]. Retrieved from http://www.hrw.org/news/2002/11/25/http://www.hrw.org/news/2002/11/25/ Guinea-security-liberian-refugees-under- threat.

CPSIA information can be obtained
at www.ICGtesting.com
Printed in the USA
FSOW04n0743040317
31429FS